FREEDOM AT NIAGARA

GERMAN-AMERICAN ACTIVISM
IN THE ABOLITION OF SLAVERY

LYNNE BREEN

WingSpan Press

Published in the United States and the United Kingdom
by WingSpan Press, Livermore, CA

The WingSpan name, logo and colophon are the trademarks of WingSpan Publishing.

ISBN 978-1-63683-496-2 (hardcover)
ISBN 978-1-63683-054-4 (pbk.)
ISBN 978-1-63683-957-8 (ebook)

First edition 2023

Printed in the United States of America

www.wingspanpress.com

Cover Image: *The Great International Railway Suspension Bridge and Niagara Falls*, hand-colored lithograph, ca. 1876. Courtesy of the Library of Congress

The publication of this book was made possible by a generous grant from the SAVA Educational Fund.

Publisher's Cataloging-in-Publication Data
Names: Breen, Lynne, author.
Title: Freedom at Niagara : German-American activism in the abolition of slavery / Lynne Breen.
Description: Includes bibliographical references. | Livermore, CA: Wingspan Press, 2023.
Identifiers: LCCN: 2023912580 | ISBN: 978-1-63683-496-2 (hardcover)
Subjects: LCSH German Americans--History--19th century. | Antislavery movements--United States--History. | Abolitionists--United States. | BISAC HISTORY / United States / 19th Century
Classification: LCC E449 .B74 2023 | DDC 326/.80922--dc23

"A German has only to be a German to be utterly opposed to slavery."

—Frederick Douglass

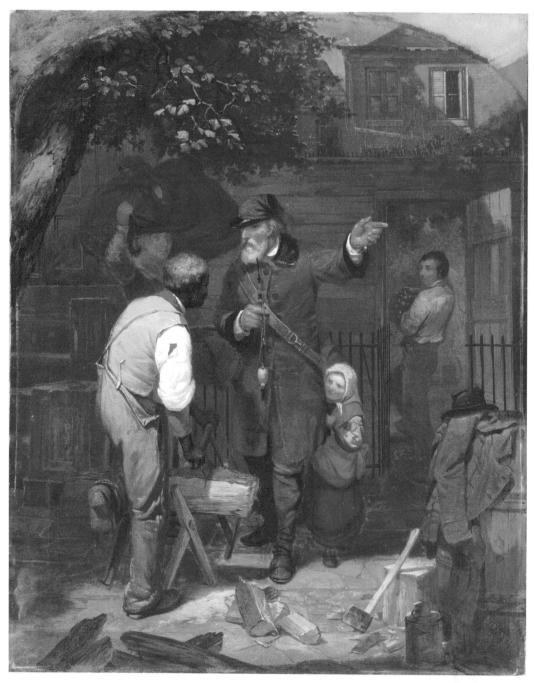

A German Immigrant Inquiring His Way, painted by American artist Charles Felix Blauvelt, 1855. The respectful demeanor of the German family, coupled with the ill-clothed yet dignified African American, captures the cordial relationship that existed between the two ethnic groups when slavery was pervasive in the United States and protected by the US Constitution.
Image courtesy of the North Carolina Museum of Art
Purchased with funds from the State of North Carolina

CONTENTS

Foreword

Two years ago, at the height of the Covid pandemic, I was privileged as Treasurer of the German-American Heritage Foundation in Washington, DC, to help publish Lynne Breen's compendium, *How German Ingenuity Inspired America: More Fun, More Beauty, More Freedom.* This beautiful coffee table book features the contributions of more than 500 Germans and German-Americans to our nation's history and culture, enriching American society over the past four centuries.

When I grew up in Saxony, Germany, I was fascinated by the universal genius of Gottfried Wilhelm Leibniz, who was born in my hometown—albeit three centuries earlier—toward the end of the Thirty Years' War. That war devastated Central Europe because of religious differences and prejudice. A polymath in mathematics, science, and philosophy, Leibniz had argued in an essay, published in 1703, that slavery defies the natural rights of humankind.

Fifty years ago, I was given the opportunity by my employer to restructure a debt-ridden company located in Commack, Long Island. Since my wife and I had just bought our first home in Berkeley Heights, New Jersey, I chose to commute the ninety-mile distance. This led me daily across New York's famous Brooklyn Bridge, designed and built by John Augustus Roebling and his family in 1869-83. Fifteen years earlier, Roebling had built the Niagara Railway Suspension Bridge.

After a decade-long effort to clean up Saxony's environmental problems in the 1990s, my wife and I moved to Philadelphia, Pennsylvania. It was here that Franz Daniel Pastorius—with William Penn's promise of religious freedom—established Germantown as the first permanent German settlement on our continent in 1683. Just five years later, Pastorius and three of his Quaker friends signed the first declaration on American soil that Africans are human beings.

For the past twenty years, I have been a Board member of the German Society of Pennsylvania, the oldest existing cultural institution in this country, dating back to colonial times. This not-for-profit organization was founded by early German settlers in Philadelphia with the aim to help immigrants—who were too poor to pay their ocean fare—from becoming indentured servants to the established British elite of the Philadelphia area.

I always enjoy walking past the historic buildings, gardens, and parks of this venerable city. Our condo building, which is located just two blocks from Penn's Landing, is called The Moravian—in memory of Count Nikolaus von Zinzendorf, who came to America from

Saxony in 1741 to establish the Moravian Church communities in Bethlehem, Pennsylvania, and Salem, North Carolina.

As President of the SAVA Educational Fund, it is my distinct pleasure to provide the necessary funding for publishing Lynne Breen's well-researched and historically important book, *Freedom at Niagara: German-American Activism in the Abolition of Slavery*. May the reader reflect on the following pages and share these historic facts with friends and neighbors.

Hardy von Auenmueller

Introduction

Harriet Tubman and John Augustus Roebling never met, but their daring feats by the mighty Niagara Falls spelled freedom for untold numbers of enslaved people running from the American South. The fervor with which the daring black abolitionist and the German-born architect chased their individual dreams is all the more wondersome as these took place in a nation that had denied citizenship to one and which looked upon the other as a foreigner.

Their actions at Niagara Falls may be regarded as the capstone of the efforts of thousands of free blacks, white abolitionists, and escaped slaves themselves to rid the United States of that most egregious of institutions—the enslavement of human beings.

Some of the loudest voices to protest slavery were those of German-Americans, the largest single ethnic group to emigrate to the United States during the early nineteenth century. They carried with them the benevolent yet scientifically proven conviction that those of African descent are equal in every way to Caucasians.

The writings of their German forebears had stirred their Teutonic souls, and when they arrived on the American continent, German immigrants were destined to join the greatest movement of civil disobedience in the United States since the Revolutionary War.

Chapter One

German Belief in the Divine Spark

Nearly seventy years after an English ship flying a Dutch flag brought the first Africans to Virginia in 1619, a newly arrived German immigrant named **Franz Daniel Pastorius** penned the first formal protest against slavery in the American colonies. That it took the Quaker conscience of Pastorius and three of his Germantown, Pennsylvania, friends to conceive such a document is a tribute to their sense of justice, for the story of slavery in America did indeed begin in Point Comfort, Virginia, just twelve years after the founding in 1607 of the first permanent British settlement in nearby Jamestown.[1]

Slavery was slow to take hold in early Virginia. From 1619, when the ship *White Lion* traded its human cargo of some twenty Africans for needed provisions, until the year 1630, the number of African slaves in Virginia colony had increased to only 59.[2]

Finding Virginia's Chesapeake area well suited to raising tobacco, English planters, at first, looked to the mother country for laborers to help cultivate the highly profitable crop. These were indentured servants, Englishmen who were "promised an infinitely better life in Virginia than they could ever hope to enjoy if they remained in Britain." Because these thousands of migrants could not afford a ship's fare to Virginia, they signed on for indentured servitude, trading five or six years of employment for the cost of their passage as well as food and clothing. Thus, by 1660, the number of Africans in Virginia accounted for just 3 or 4 percent of the colony's population, numbering only 950.[3]

During the final quarter of the seventeenth century, however, the employment picture shifted from indentured servitude to primarily enslaved labor. Conditions in England were improving, and other American colonies, such as Pennsylvania, were vying for the dwindling number of indentured British servants. As a result, tobacco planters in Virginia were eager to do business with transatlantic slave traders to acquire the workers they needed.[4]

Virginia was not the only colony of the original thirteen to exploit slave labor. Among the southern colonies, planters in Maryland began to purchase slaves rather than indentured servants beginning in the 1660s.[5] Slavery was legally sanctioned in Carolina as early as 1669. In 1729, when the colony was officially divided into North and South, slavery had been flourishing in the region for sixty years.

Depiction of Virginia tobacco cultivation at Jamestown, ca. 1615.

Georgia was the only colony to formally ban slavery, which it did in 1735, two years after its first settlers arrived. However, the colony's trustees capitulated in 1751 when the planter class intensified its arguments for allowing slavery. In 1755, Georgia approved the first slave code drafted by its own residents, using a 1740 South Carolina slave act as a model.[6]

Heavily dependent on African slaves to work their tobacco and rice plantations, the southern colonies thus became "slave societies"—where labor was defined by the existence of a master class and a slave class. Between 1730 and 1775, more than one-third of the total population of the southern colonies was enslaved: North Carolina, about 25 percent; Maryland, more than 30 percent; Virginia, about 40 percent; and South Carolina, possibly more than 60 percent.[7]

Just as Maryland farmers had done in the late 1600s, farmers in the grain-producing economies of Pennsylvania, New Jersey, and New York during the 1700s turned from British indentured servants to African slaves.[8] In Delaware, where the Dutch West India Company made quick inroads, the enslaved eventually comprised 20 percent of the colony's total population, while in New York, the percentage was somewhat lower at 14 percent, and in Pennsylvania and New Jersey, about 8 percent.[9]

Map of the Original Thirteen Colonies, 1775.

New Englanders did not view slavery as central to their agricultural economies because of a shorter growing season,[10] but all four colonies—Connecticut, Massachusetts, New Hampshire, and Rhode Island—were dependent on the slave trade for commercial success in shipbuilding and commerce, profiting from these ventures by sending "thousands of ships to Africa where they purchased local captives who were then transported across the Atlantic and sold in the Caribbean or Southern colonies and states."[11]

Still, slavery in New England accounted for just 3 percent of its total population as the majority of masters could afford only one or two slaves to assist with household chores and the operation of a small farm or business.[12] While the African slave population in the North remained appreciably lower than in the South, slavery in all of Britain's North American colonies continued to grow, from fewer than 3,000 in 1660 to nearly 7,000 in 1680.[13]

Monument dedicated to Franz Daniel Pastorius (1651-1720) and the first German Quakers who settled in Germantown, Philadelphia, in 1683.

Just three years later, Germantown, on the eastern boundary of Pennsylvania, became the first permanent German settlement in the British colonies. Franz Daniel Pastorius and a "handful" of other emigrants arrived in 1683 from the town of Krefeld, Germany. Within just five years of the town's founding, Pastorius wrote in English, and he and three Quaker friends signed, the Germantown Quaker Petition Against Slavery—the first declaration on American soil that Africans are human beings. The petition was based on the belief that the Golden Rule invalidated human bondage through the simple clarity of its words: "Do unto others as you would have others do unto you."[14]

The Germantown Quaker Petition Against Slavery was written in 1688 at the home of Thones Kunders (ca. 1654-1729) in Germantown, Pennsylvania. The petition was based on the belief that the Golden Rule invalidated human bondage through the simple clarity of its words, "Do unto others as you would have others do unto you."

This momentous event foreshadowed German inquiry into the nature of what it is to be human. In 1703 and 1775, when **Gottfried Wilhelm Leibniz** and **Johann Friedrich Blumenbach** set forth theories, respectively, that challenged the prevailing European attitude that Africans are an inferior race, the Teutonic belief in the divine spark[15] became evident.

Leibniz, considered a polymath for his proficiency in mathematics, science, and philosophy as well as in diplomacy, focused on the moral status of slavery in his 1703 essay "On the Common Notion of Justice," arguing that slavery defies the natural rights of humankind. Leibniz believed that "all human beings have a special moral status, partly due to their place in God's plan and partly due to their capacity for rationality."[16]

Portrait of German polymath Gottfried Wilhelm Leibniz (1646-1716) by German painter Christoph Bernhard Francke, 1695. Image courtesy of the Herzog Anton Ulrich Museum, Braunschweig, Germany

Blumenbach entered the controversy in 1775, the year he was awarded a medical degree from the University of Göttingen. In his dissertation *On the Natural Varieties of Mankind*, he renounced racism and slavery, arguing that differences in physical constitution, stature, and color were "owing almost entirely to climate alone . . . that colour, whatever be its causes . . . can never constitute a diversity of species."[17]

He continued: "I do not see the slightest shadow of reason why I, looking at the matter from a physiological and scientific point of view, should have any doubt whatever that all nations, under all known climates, belong to one and exactly the same common species."[18]

Portrait of Johann Friedrich Blumenbach (1752-1840) by German painter
Ludwig Emil Grimm, 1823. Image courtesy of the British Museum

Reflecting on the early pronouncements of these learned men, it was thus inevitable that German-Americans in the century ahead would become allies of free and enslaved blacks and white abolitionists in a common effort to eradicate the hated institution of slavery.

Chapter Two

An Untenable Constitution in a New Land

When James Madison, father of the United States Constitution, was eight years old, his grandmother presented him with a young slave named Billey. In the years following, Madison inherited additional slaves so that, by 1787, at the age of 36, he was the master of sixteen enslaved people. Madison publicly said he did not wish to rely on the labor of slaves, yet his livelihood, throughout his lifetime, was dependent on slavery.[19]

Portrait of James Madison (1751-1836) of Virginia by John Vanderlyn, 1816. Madison was fourth US president, from 1809 to 1817. Image courtesy of the White House Historical Association

Madison's contradiction between thought and behavior serves as a metaphor for the cognitive dissonance displayed by nearly all of the founding fathers with regard to slavery. Even before the Treaty of Paris in 1783 ended the American Revolutionary War, dissolving British ownership of the thirteen colonies,[20] the acceptance of slavery clashed with the wish to establish a utopian government based on the ideals of liberty and democracy.

The majority of planters who owned slaves embraced the Revolutionary War, condemning the autocratic crown of Britain while defending the "rights of man."[21] Patriots from throughout the colonies blustered they "were remaking the world," and, in 1776, the language of the Declaration of Independence bolstered the patriots' high opinion of themselves "as holding the moral, philosophical, and political high ground."[22]

Writing the Declaration of Independence, 1776 by American artist Jean Leon Gerome Ferris. Left to right: Benjamin Franklin (1705-1790), John Adams (1735-1826), and Thomas Jefferson (1743-1826). Image courtesy of the Virginia Historical Society

Yet the American economy was based on the enormous wealth produced by slave labor, particularly in the southern states, where tobacco, rice, sugar, and cotton crops were sold on the international market. In the early days of the republic, four of the first five presidents owned slaves—**George Washington**, **Thomas Jefferson**, **James Madison**, and **James Monroe**.

Further, slave masters of the planting classes in Virginia and Maryland and into the Deep South held a majority in Congress.[23]

In 1774, before the onset of the Revolutionary War, the Continental Congress[24] banned the importation of slaves from Britain. However, the measure was intended as a trade embargo against an adversary rather than a humanitarian act. Still, a more aggressive antislavery movement began to surface during the 1770s as Methodist, Baptist, and Quaker dignitaries roused the public conscience through sermons, printed tracts, lawsuits, and the petitioning of legislatures.[25]

A common antislavery attitude among Quakers did not come easily. Until the 1750s, most members of the Society of Friends held no opinion of slavery or were slave owners themselves—farmers who found slave labor practical and who stood firm against abandoning the practice. Over the years, however, individual Friends began to persuade fellow parishioners that slavery was contrary to Quaker beliefs in nonviolence and the equality of all individuals in the eyes of God, giving rise to formidable abolition societies in Pennsylvania and elsewhere.[26]

At the same time, northern colonies were beginning to wrestle with the conclusion that slavery was inherently evil, adopting laws that forbade the practice. In 1780, Pennsylvania passed the Gradual Abolition Act, authorizing Pennsylvanians to maintain the slaves they already owned and allowing for the eventual freedom of those newly born into slavery.[27] This legislation was followed up by Massachusetts, which outlawed slavery by judicial decree in 1783; New Hampshire, which began a gradual abolition of slavery in the same year; and Connecticut and Rhode Island, whose governing bodies passed gradual abolition acts in 1784.[28]

The stage was thus set for a confrontation on the slavery question at the Constitutional Convention, where 55 delegates from twelve states[29] met in Philadelphia in 1787—four years after the Revolutionary War had ended. George Washington of Virginia, hero of that war, was elected to preside at the assembly. In drafting what would become the supreme law of the land, the daunting task at hand was forging a compromise on the slavery issue, with delegates from the northern states viewing democracy and slavery as incongruous and southern state delegates determined to preserve the shameful practice.

In this atmosphere, few delegates at the convention wanted to take up the slavery issue or even mention the word; consequently, the word "slave" cannot be found anywhere in the original Constitution. However, an agreement *was* reached on how to determine a state's population with respect to slavery. Called the Three-Fifths Compromise, the measure specified that three-fifths of a state's slave population would be counted in allocating that state's quota of seats in the US House of Representatives. But, even here, the founders sidestepped the word "slave," referring to enslaved individuals instead as "all other Persons."[30]

The Three-Fifths Compromise was emblematic of the deep division in the fledgling nation as its adoption gave the slave-holding southern states disproportionately greater representation in the House of Representatives—and thus enormous political clout.[31] Northern delegates had acquiesced, knowing that without such an agreement, delegates from South Carolina and Georgia might "refuse to join the Union."[32]

Scene at the Signing of the Constitution of the United States by American artist Howard Chandler Christy, showing George Washington (1732-1799) presiding over the assembly at the Pennsylvania State House in Philadelphia. Image courtesy of the United States Capitol

The Constitution reinforced slavery in other ways as well: prohibiting Congress from banning the African slave trade before 1808; prohibiting the taxation of exports produced primarily from slave labor; assuring federal intervention in the event of slave uprisings; and asserting that only citizens could access the federal court system. And, because the Constitution established a federal government of limited powers, Congress lacked the authority to become involved in the internal affairs of individual states.[33]

Indeed, noted German zoologist **Dr. Johann David Schöpf**, who traveled throughout the United States in 1783 and 1784, observed the sharp contrast between North and South in attitudes toward human enslavement, predicting that the slavery argument would develop into a major issue for America.[34]

In contrast to the Constitution, the Northwest Ordinance—also adopted by Congress in 1787—sought to limit slavery when it created the Northwest Territory from lands north of the Ohio River and from the Appalachian Mountains west to the Mississippi River.[35] Article VI of the Ordinance stated: "There shall be neither Slavery nor involuntary Servitude in the said territory . . . ."

Paradoxically, Article VI also declared: ". . . provided always that any person escaping into the same, from whom labor or service is lawfully claimed in any one of the original States, such fugitive may be lawfully reclaimed and conveyed to the person claiming his or her labor or service as aforesaid"—clearly endorsing slavery by authorizing slave masters to capture fugitives who had escaped to the Northwest Territory.

While **Abraham Lincoln** in future years would credit the Ordinance for keeping slavery out of the Northwest, its stipulations had no immediate effect. Slavery in the region continued for decades because of its deep-rooted history as well as the unwillingness of local and federal officials to enforce the ordinance.[36]

Portrait of William Henry Harrison (1773-1841) of Virginia by American artist Rembrandt Peale, ca. 1813. Image courtesy of the Smithsonian National Portrait Gallery

Moreover, **William Henry Harrison**, appointed secretary of the Northwest Territory in 1798, just two years later was named governor of the Indiana Territory, where his first major undertaking was to bring more slaves into the region. With an aristocratic Virginia upbringing—and, facing a labor shortage in Indiana Territory—Harrison petitioned the US Congress in 1802 to permit slavery in the territory. Congress, however, denied Harrison's request. In 1816, when Indiana entered the Union, it did so as a free state.[37]

A Visit from the Distinguished German Explorer

In 1804, Thomas Jefferson was in the third year of his presidency when he hosted a visit from **Alexander von Humboldt**, the renowned German explorer and naturalist who had studied at the University of Göttingen with **Johann Friedrich Blumenbach**.[38]

It is not known whether the freedom-minded Humboldt discussed the slavery issue with Jefferson. He did, however, provide Jefferson with important maps and statistics, revamping American cartography at a critical time: The President in 1803 had signed the Louisiana Purchase with France, adding to the young nation 827,000 square miles of land west of the Mississippi River. A new, detailed US map that Humboldt had constructed and shared with Jefferson has been said to be the most consequential contribution the German scientist made to America.[39]

Portrait of Alexander von Humboldt (1769-1859) by German painter Friedrich Georg Weitsch, 1806. Image courtesy of the Alte Nationalgalerie, Berlin, Germany

An ardent supporter of the United States, Humboldt often referred to himself as "half-American," yet the nation's economic dependence on slavery caused him considerable anguish. Like others who believed in the ideals of liberty and democracy, Humboldt hoped that when the Constitution's moratorium on the African slave trade ended in 1808, the country would take the necessary steps to abolish slavery.[40]

Sadly, the demand for slaves would multiply in the years ahead,[41] with no end in sight of the malevolent institution.

Chapter Three

Sanctioned Slavery: An Inescapable Truth

A fragile sense of optimism filled the chilly winter air in 1807 as Congress voted to abolish the African slave trade, to be effective one year later, on January 1, 1808. As of that date, Americans no longer would be permitted to do business with African slave traders, whose captives in years past were readily accepted on the Atlantic shore. For most northerners—and for others who detested slavery—the end of the slave trade promised a republic where slavery would gradually fade into extinction.

The United States, however, was already too reliant on the institution for it to be easily swept away. Large plantations in Maryland and Virginia as well as those in the Deep South required hundreds of thousands of slave laborers to cultivate tobacco, rice, and cotton crops for both national and international trade. The immense profits from these agricultural ventures served to define the planter class, who viewed their slaves as valuable assets—possibly more valuable than the land itself.[42]

The Cotton Pickers, by American painter Winslow Homer, 1876.
Image courtesy of the Los Angeles County Museum of Art

In 1794, the invention of the cotton gin reinvigorated the growing of cotton, as Eli Whitney's newly patented machine made it easier—and thus more efficient—to separate cotton fibers from their seeds. Cotton productivity soared and, with it, enormous profits. In the 1780s, the American colonies were producing fewer than 1 percent of the world's cotton. By 1810, this figure stood at more than 53 percent, and, by 1861, states south of the Mason-Dixon Line were producing fully 80 percent of the world's cotton crop.[43]

With the closing of the African slave trade in 1808, planters began to consider the well-being of their existing slaves, especially the health of female slaves in their child-bearing years. Slave owners generally assigned less strenuous tasks and allotted extra food to slaves who were pregnant. Thus, an estimated 400,000 individuals who had been imported from Africa would swell to some four million by 1860.[44]

In the early 1800s, farmers in the mid-Atlantic—their tobacco fields depleted because of short-sighted agricultural practices—began diversifying their crops, often selling their slaves to planters in cotton-rich states or freeing them en masse. Also, a number of slaves who had enlisted to fight in the Revolutionary War were given their freedom at war's end. Further, former slave owners in the North, rethinking their perspective on the slavery issue, manumitted their charges, as did those moved by the evangelical pleas of Quakers and those of other denominations.[45]

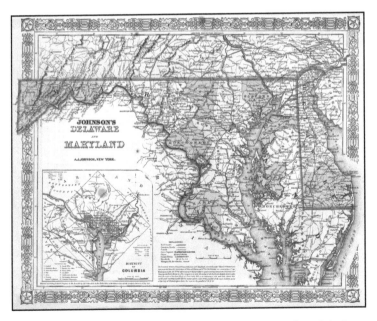

A hand-colored map of Delaware and Maryland published in 1864 by Alvin Jewett Johnson's atlas printing company, New York City. Created during the Civil War, the map shows the horizontal line between Pennsylvania and Maryland called the Mason-Dixon Line—considered the boundary between the free northern states and the slaveholding southern states.

This escalating number of free blacks led to the heinous practice of kidnapping newly freed persons and returning them to slavery—yet another avenue for increasing the planter's slave roster. Although illegal in most states, the crime was committed against black people in a society controlled by whites. Kidnappers were thus aware they could operate with little risk, generally taking their captives by force or through threats of violence. Free blacks living in states just north and south of the Mason-Dixon Line—Pennsylvania, Delaware, and Maryland—were particularly vulnerable as they were in close proximity to the South and could be quickly transported on land, or by boat down the Delaware River.[46]

In stark contrast to the grandiose lives of southern plantation owners were the lives of the enslaved, considered little more than property by the patrician ruling class. Most slaves worked in the cotton fields—as many as fourteen hours a day during the oppressive heat of summer and an average of ten in the biting cold of winter. Those who worked in rice fields faced misery as well, obliged to stand for hours in water up to their knees as they tended the subaquatic crop.[47]

Family of slaves on the plantation of William Gaines, Hanover
County, Virginia, 1862. Image courtesy of the Library of Congress

The physical requirements of house slaves were considerably less demanding than those of field hands—consisting of cooking, cleaning, sewing, and serving as laundresses and nursemaids. Further, they could expect better food and clothing. But working in the master's house could be mentally exhausting as house servants were under constant close supervision, expected to be on call at any hour of the night, and more apt to become entangled in personal conflicts with their white masters, leading to whippings and even sexual assaults.[48]

Forced sexual relations with enslaved black women was not uncommon, for there was no law making it a crime. The frequency with which such abuse occurred was made obvious by the thousands of mulatto children living on southern plantations.[49] The enslaved **Harriet Jacobs** recalled: "There is a great difference between Christianity and religion [in] the south," she wrote. "If a pastor has offspring by a woman not his wife, the church dismiss him, if she is a white woman; but if she is colored, it does not hinder his continuing to be their good shepherd."[50]

Physical cruelties were broadly expected in the laboring fields, where slaves were often supervised by boorish overseers, whose "capricious violence and malice compounded the miseries of work in an unforgiving environment."[51] While slaveholders more often fired overseers for treating their slaves too abusively, masters also were known to dismiss unduly lenient overseers, who had been entrusted to maximize the plantation's profits.[52]

Brutish acts carried out by slave masters were generally overlooked by neighboring planters as they, too, used force and threats of bodily harm. Punishments ranged from being whipped for leaving the plantation without the required pass to being lynched for killing a white person, even in self-defense. Any type of rebelliousness could result in a slave being strangled, burned, or shackled.[53]

Slaves picking cotton in the American South while being
watched by a white overseer on horseback, ca. 1850.

Slave patrollers—equipped with guns, binding ropes, and whips—were yet another means to ensure that black people remained submissive and defenseless. Taken from the lower classes of society, slave patrollers were given the authority to both berate and punish the enslaved.

They tormented blacks for offenses ranging from lingering outside after curfew and stealing food to hiding weapons and congregating without a white person present.[54]

Slave men and women used the coping mechanisms of silence and sabotage to endure the despair they faced as human property, hoping to keep their masters oblivious to the hatred and anger they felt. Retaliation took the form of work slow downs, vandalizing wagons, pulling down fences, breaking farm equipment, "losing" tools by pitching them into a river, pretending not to understand instructions, and serving spoiled food.[55]

None of these acts, however, could erase the slave's greatest fear: that of being sold to a master in a distant place and thus separated forever from his or her family. Even the death of a plantation owner was cause for alarm as it raised the likelihood that slaves would be sold—in addition to the possibility that a slave might be sent to the far-off plantation of an heir, where familiar bonds would be severed with as much certainty as an actual sale.[56]

In *Sold to Go South*, an enslaved man bids goodbye to his wife and child. From *The Suppressed Book about Slavery!*, published in 1864.

While slaves toiling on highly profitable plantations were less likely to be sold than those working on small farms, the number of sales transactions in the seven decades leading up to the Civil War was still formidable: One slave family in five was torn apart by separation and sale, and one child in three was cut off from his or her parents.[57]

Little hope was on the horizon that slavery would end in a nation whose Congress and presidency, for the most part, were controlled by proslavery southerners. This was evidenced as early as 1820, when Congress enacted the Missouri Compromise, which admitted the new state of Missouri as a slave state and Maine as a free state. While the Compromise maintained the nation's balance between slave and free states, that slavery was extended westward prompted a bitter reaction.[58]

The heat of the measure's debate in Congress reached such a high pitch that it confirmed the deep divide that existed between proslavery and antislavery forces—southern representatives wanting slavery extended to the West, and northern representatives just as vehemently opposed to its spread. And, because it did not resolve the question of what should be done about slavery, the Missouri Compromise put off for a whole generation a decisive action to mend America's tragic flaw.[59]

Portrait of German-born abolitionist Charles Follen (1796-1840), 1844.

Among the outraged northerners was German-born **Charles Follen**, dismissed from his teaching post at Harvard for his staunch abolitionist views. Public controversy over an impassioned speech he had delivered earlier before the New England Anti-Slavery Society is said to be the reason for his ouster. After leaving the university, Follen became ordained as a minister and, in 1838, accepted a post at a Unitarian church in New York City, only to be dismissed again for alienating the parishioners with what was considered his radical abolitionism.[60]

Clearly, Follen—who had embraced his generation's German ideals of liberty and freedom—was ahead of his time in his adopted country, which continued to accept slavery as a necessary evil.

Chapter Four

Complicity in the Capital City

U nder the watchful eye of foremen and overseers, slaves imported from Africa cut the quarry stone and moved it to the White House building site. Later, using bricks that had been baked in onsite kilns and lumber from trees felled in Maryland and Virginia, they worked with care alongside paid laborers as they set the exterior walls in place, for this was going to be the President's House, a symbol of freedom in a nation conceived in liberty.

The inconsistency between the ideals of the new republic and using slave labor to build the executive mansion in Washington, DC, apparently went unnoticed by the building planners—commissioners selected by President George Washington in 1791 to oversee the building of the White House as well as the Capitol Building. Like thirteen of the first fifteen presidents, the original three commissioners owned slaves.[61]

East front elevation of the "President's House" by architect Benjamin Henry Latrobe (1764-1820), 1807. Latrobe was responsible for the completion of both the Capitol and the White House. Image courtesy of the Library of Congress

The symbolism of this historical event suggests not only a common disregard in the capital city for the rights of African Americans, but a disregard as well for these rights across an entire nation. The mission of the Federal City should have been to shine a beacon of liberty across the land, independent from the states, slave or free.

Instead, **George Washington**, **Thomas Jefferson**, and **James Madison**, all founding fathers from Virginia, maneuvered to establish the capital city in the South, not only for the esteem and monetary benefits it would bring, but also to safeguard slavery—the basis of the southern economy.[62]

Southerners worried that placing the capital in the North would threaten the institution of slavery and ultimately weaken southern influence in Congress. Petitions pressing for an end to the slave trade from Quakers as well as from the Pennsylvania Abolition Society served only to reinforce southern resolve to place the Federal City in the slaveholding South, leading to the Residence Act of 1790.[63]

This law gave President Washington full authority to select a location. He chose a spot along the Potomac River—fewer than two miles from his Mount Vernon estate—with Maryland and Virginia agreeing to transfer the prescribed land. At the time, more than half of the slaves in the country—396,000 adults and children—lived in these two states.[64]

Pierre Charles L'Enfant's plan for Washington, DC, 1792, as revised by Andrew Ellicott. Image courtesy of the Library of Congress

In November 1800, the Federal Government officially made its move from New York City to Washington, DC, a time when the new seat of government was publicized as "a citadel of liberty"—even though nearly 85 percent of black residents were slaves. In 1808, the same year in which the Constitution ended US participation in the African slave trade, Washington, DC, instituted its first black codes, revealing that the city had indeed been founded on discrimination.[65]

This was evidenced as early as 1791, when the boundaries of the new Federal City were drawn. A surveyor named **Andrew Ellicott** was hired, whose assistant was a free African American named **Benjamin Banneker**. It was Banneker who determined the position of the first boundary stone at Jones Point, on the southern tip of Alexandria, by lying on the bare ground at night and calculating the motion of six stars.[66]

The fact that Banneker was an Ethiopian prompted an editorial comment in the *Georgetown Weekly Ledger*, pointing out that Jefferson—instrumental in placing the capital city in the South—considered African Americans an inferior race: Banneker's "abilities, as a surveyor and an astronomer," noted the editorial, "clearly prove that Mr. Jefferson's concluding that race of men were void of mental endowments was without foundation."[67]

Later, Banneker himself wrote to Jefferson, praising his writing of the Declaration of Independence, though decrying the founding father's hypocrisy: "But, Sir, how pitiable is it to reflect that although you were so fully convinced of the benevolence of the Father of mankind, and of his equal and impartial distribution of those rights and privileges which he had conferred upon them, that you should at the same time counteract his mercies, in detaining by fraud and violence so numerous a part of my brethren under groaning captivity and cruel oppression."[68]

"Benjamin Banneker: Surveyor-Inventor-Astronomer" mural by American artist Maxime Seelbinder, at the Recorder of Deeds building in Washington, DC. Image courtesy of the Library of Congress

Hence, the Federal City's slave codes, adopted just seventeen years later, prohibited people of color from being outside after 10 p.m. and from dancing, playing ball, drinking, or arguing. Disobeying slaves whose masters refused to pay the $5 fine were to be whipped. In 1812, the codes were strengthened, with errant slaves subject to up to forty lashes, and free blacks required to register with the city and carry proof of their freedom.[69]

These codes were in addition to the slave laws of Maryland and Virginia, which extended to the nation's capital. Maryland's laws stipulated that slaves could give testimony against another slave, but not against a white person, and slaves who lied in court were subject to thirty-nine lashes and having their ears cut off. Those caught running away could be branded with an "R."[70]

Regardless of social class, the white population in the Federal City relied on African Americans to perform domestic work, with nearly 40 percent of Washington households owning slaves. While their chores did not appear to be unduly burdensome, house servants lived in constant fear of being sold to a master in the agricultural South, where life was considerably harsher.[71]

Portrait of James Monroe (1758-1831) of Virginia by American artist Samuel F. B. Morse, ca. 1819. The fifth US President, Monroe served two terms, from 1817 to 1825. Image courtesy of the White House Historical Association

John Quincy Adams (1767-1848) of Massachusetts was one of only two presidents before
Lincoln to find slavery reprehensible. This portrait of Adams was painted in 1858 by American
artist George Peter Alexander Healy. A daguerreotype of the sixth president—the first
photograph of a US chief executive—was achieved in 1843 by German-born lithographer
Philip Haas (ca. 1808-1863). Image courtesy of the White House Historical Society

Such fears were not unfounded. With just trees and expanses of grass on the one-and-
a-half-mile-stretch between the White House and the Capitol, no effort was required to see
slaves being shepherded to the Potomac River docks, where they would board ships waiting
to take them to auction in the Deep South, principally New Orleans, which fetched the highest
prices.[72]

Other slaves were escorted toward the National Mall, where slave pens had been positioned
around the perimeter. One of the most notorious was the "Yellow House," where slave-owning
visitors to Washington, DC, could house their human property temporarily for twenty-five
cents a day. More often, however, the owner—William H. Williams—would buy and sell
enslaved men, women, and children on speculation, hoping to buy low in the nation's capital
and sell high in the South.[73]

The Captive Slave by British portrait painter John Simpson,
1827. First exhibited in London, the painting was intended as an
abolitionist statement. Image courtesy of the Art Institute of Chicago

Conditions at the Yellow House were so atrocious that Quaker poet and abolitionist John Greenleaf Whittier lamented "the dreadful amount of human agony and suffering" that characterized the jail. He also noted that one of its "secret horrors" was the occasional suicide of an inmate who had lost all hope.[74]

While the Yellow House looked no different from other houses in Washington, DC, the enslaved were also held—and sold—in commercial buildings along Pennsylvania Avenue, the corridor connecting the Capitol Building to the White House. With their owners' strong encouragement, the St. Charles Hotel and the United States Hotel were used as slave pens, as were Lafayette Tavern and the Decatur House, located just two blocks east of the White House. Brazenly, at Center Market—on Seventh Street and Pennsylvania Avenue—white patrons could purchase slaves at the same time as their groceries.[75]

SCENE IN THE SLAVE PEN AT WASHINGTON.

Scene in the Slave Pen at Washington, published in
1853. Image courtesy of the New York Public Library

A German-Born Editor and Freedom of Speech

A newspaper editor, German-born John Peter Zenger is credited with laying the foundation for the First Amendment to the US Constitution when he went on trial in 1735 for defaming the British Colonial Governor of New York. Zenger was acquitted when his attorney, Andrew Hamilton, established truth as a defense against libel. Speaking to the jury, Hamilton said: "It is not the Cause of the poor Printer, nor of New York alone, which you are now trying; No! It may in its Consequence, affect every Freeman that lives under a British Government on the main of America. It is the best Cause. It is the Cause of Liberty; and I make no Doubt but your upright Conduct, this Day, will not only entitle you to the Love and Esteem of your Fellow-Citizens; but every Man who prefers Freedom to a Life of slavery will bless and honour You …."[76]

One hundred years later, President **Andrew Jackson** violated the First Amendment by calling for the suppression of abolitionist literature. In July 1835, the American Anti-Slavery

Society launched a massive mail campaign by flooding the Charleston, South Carolina, post office with abolitionist literature. Incensed by this action, the slave-owning president called the tracts "unconstitutional and wicked," and, in his annual message to Congress that December, asked for a law to prohibit the mailing of such "incendiary publications, intended to instigate the slaves to insurrection."[77] Wisely, Congress did not adopt Jackson's recommendation.

Portrait of Andrew Jackson (1767-1845) of Tennessee by American painter Ralph Eleaser Whiteside Earl, ca. 1835. The seventh US president, Jackson served two terms, from 1829 to 1837. Image courtesy of the White House Historical Society

Chapter Five

Enlightenment in the British Commonwealth

When French explorer **Jacques Cartier** discovered the Gulf of Saint Lawrence in 1534, he claimed the territory—now known as Canada—for King **Francis I**. Even though slavery was prohibited in the colony, just as it was in France, in 1709 King **Louis XIV** allowed farmers and fur traders to import slaves to New France to assist with clearing the land and to perform domestic chores for the wealthier inhabitants.[78]

By the time Britain wrested control of Canada in 1763 at the conclusion of the Seven Years' War, Britannia had been involved in the transatlantic slave trade for more than 200 years and was its dominant player. And, because New France had been importing slaves since the early 1700s, Britain's only challenge was to anglicize the French settlement. By 1784, more than 1,800 slaves were living in the territory.[79]

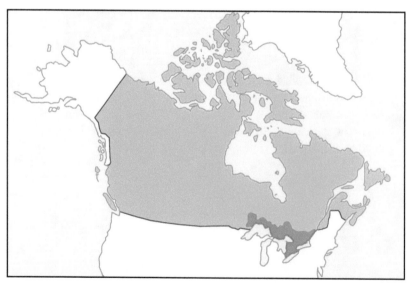

The Province of Upper Canada, shown in orange, was so named because of its location north of the Great Lakes. The province was renamed Ontario in 1867, two years after the end of the American Civil War.

Two communities were established in Canada along the Niagara River: one located south along the river to the Welland River; the other, west from the Niagara River across the Ontario Plain, an area that stretches from the southeastern shore of Lake Erie to the southern shore of Lake Ontario. Many of the early settlers were from the thirteen American colonies—British loyalists who preferred to live under the Royal Crown following its defeat in the Revolutionary War. Some brought their slaves with them.[80]

In 1791, the British Government renamed the territory the Province of Upper Canada, "upper" referring to its location north of the Great Lakes. **John Graves Simcoe**, a British Army general, became the first lieutenant governor of Upper Canada, and it was he who engineered the removal of slavery from the Province.[81] Born in England, Simcoe had supported the abolishment of slavery even before becoming lieutenant governor of Upper Canada.

Portrait of John Graves Simcoe (1752-1806) by French artist George Théodore Berthon, ca. 1881. Image courtesy of the Government of Ontario Art Collection

An avowed abolitionist, Simcoe in 1793 introduced a bill to prohibit slavery in Upper Canada, only to be challenged by slave-holding cabinet members. A compromise thus ensued representing a gradual approach to ending slavery: The Act to Limit Slavery specified that those who were enslaved at the signing of the bill would remain the property of their owners for life. It also allowed the sale of slaves to continue within the Province. Further, it allowed slave owners to pursue and apprehend runaways within Upper Canada.[82]

However, the act *did* forbid anyone to import slaves into the Province, and, further, stipulated that children born to slaves after 1793 would gain their freedom when they reached the age of twenty-five. The children of these children would be free at birth.[83]

In contrast to the American colonies, the number of slaves in Upper Canada remained small. With a short growing season, the expense of feeding, clothing, and housing slaves throughout an unprofitable winter was viewed as impractical. Further, the Province did not have a need for overseers or regulatory controls such as black codes, and reports were rare that a slave had been treated inhumanely. In some instances, the enslaved were freed on the condition of remaining with their owner as a paid servant.[84]

While the 1793 act did not end the practice of slavery, it helped change public opinion about the morality of the institution. Also significant was the effect of Simcoe's act upon public attitudes on the other side of the Atlantic. His legacy is said to have established the framework for the abolition of slavery across the entire British Commonwealth. As one would assume, Simcoe was an avid supporter of **William Wilberforce**, the Britisher who became a hero among antislavery advocates calling for an end to the despicable practice.[85]

Portrait of British abolitionist William Wilberforce (1759-1833), ca. 1790. His birthplace is now a British historic house museum in Kingston upon Hull, East Riding of Yorkshire. Wilberforce was buried at Westminster Abbey, the traditional burial site for British monarchs.

Born in Yorkshire, England, in 1759, Wilberforce was elected to Parliament in 1784 and, one year later, became an evangelical Christian, leading him to believe that "abolition was indeed that single cause to which God was calling him in Parliament." Though suffering from ill health for much of his life, Wilberforce waged a twenty-year battle against the proslavery forces in Parliament, finally achieving victory with the Slavery Abolition Act of 1833.[86] So revered in England, Wilberforce was buried at Westminster Abbey, the traditional burial site for British monarchs.

As in Upper Canada in 1783, the British law was a compromise: Slaves seven years of age and older who labored in the fields were to be apprenticed to their former owners for a period of six years, after which they would be freed. Slaves working in other capacities would serve a four-year apprenticeship; children up to six years old were granted complete freedom; and former slave masters were to be compensated for the loss of their human property.[87]

The painting *Slave in Chains*, ca. 1820—representing the misery endured by enslaved Africans during their transatlantic voyage—was widely distributed by European abolitionists to arouse compassion for those in bondage. Image courtesy of the Royal Museums Greenwich

Taking effect on August 1, 1834, the Act abolished slavery in nearly all of Britain's colonies, including those in British North America. The new law thus made Upper Canada—indeed, all of Canada—a free territory for fugitive slaves from the United States.

The Teutonic Love of Liberty

In 1832, British historian and archivist **Sir Francis Palgrave** proclaimed in *Rise and Progress of the English Commonwealth* that the English had acquired their ideas of government from the Romans and the Teutons, "from Rome the idea of monarchy . . . and from the Teutons the idea of limiting the power of the monarch." Palgrave noted that "the love of liberty with definite safeguards against arbitrary power had always been characteristic of the Teutonic forebears."[88]

Portrait of Sir Francis Palgrave (1788-1861) by British artist Mary Dawson Turner, 1823.

Chapter Six

An Anxious Nation

B y the time **Martin Van Buren** became president in 1837, it was apparent the United States was headed toward a cataclysmic solution to the slavery issue. That slavery would disappear eventually on its own accord, as the founding fathers had believed,[89] revealed their naiveté or, perhaps, a willingness to put off for generations a firm resolution to what was now a crisis.

Portrait of Martin Van Buren (1782-1862) of New York by American artist George Peter Alexander Healy, 1858. The eighth US president, Van Buren served for one term, from 1837 to 1841. Image courtesy of the White House Historical Association

Six years earlier, America had witnessed one of the bloodiest insurrections in its young history. **Nat Turner**, a slave in southern Virginia, gathered a band of slaves and led a two-day killing spree that resulted in the deaths of some sixty white people. Retaliation was swift, with white people killing twice that many black people. Turner escaped, but eventually was caught, convicted, and hanged.[90]

In reaction, the South resurrected its fear of slave uprisings, as more than half of the southern population was now enslaved. Planters went to bed each night apprehensively, terror-stricken at the thought of what could happen next.[91]

Nat Turner & His Confederates in Conference. Image courtesy of the New York Public Library

While South Carolina and Georgia had passed anti-literacy laws—prohibiting teaching slaves how to read and write—prior to Turner's mutiny, additional southern states began enacting such measures, fearful that antislavery tracts would incite further slave revolts. It infuriated slaveholders that much of the abolitionist literature being disseminated throughout the South contained visual clues, undermining their efforts to keep slaves illiterate.[92]

Freedom of speech was a crucial weapon in the arsenal of abolitionists, who refused to be daunted by proslavery factions. Bostonian **William Lloyd Garrison** published the first edition of *The Liberator* on January 1, 1831, after telling a group of black leaders that his abolitionist newspaper would support them by affirming their character and fighting for their rights. Despite receiving threatening letters from southern slaveowners, Garrison published his weekly newspaper for thirty-five years, the last issue dated December 29, 1865.[93]

Photograph of William Lloyd Garrison (1805-1879), 1870. Image courtesy of the Library of Congress

In 1833, when the American Anti-Slavery Society was founded, its members overwhelmed Congress with hundreds of thousands of petitions appealing for an end to slavery. Further, the society in 1839 published 100,000 copies of *American Slavery As It Is: Testimony of a Thousand Witnesses*, a scrupulously documented volume that exposed the agonizing forms of torture inflicted on the enslaved.[94]

Roused by the prodding petitions, the expansion of slavery westward, and Britain's recent measure to end the practice, a few antislavery Congressmen raised the subject of human bondage, only to be met with southern-imposed gag rules that forbade its discussion on the House floor. Members of Congress from slave-holding states were also becoming more combative in their defense of the practice: Between 1830 and 1860, more than seventy fiery exchanges took place in congressional chambers and on the streets of Washington.[95]

Further, it had not been forgotten that President Van Buren had been in favor of giving free blacks the franchise in 1821, even though he promised in his 1837 inaugural speech that he would never meddle with slavery. Southerners simply did not trust this president from the North.[96]

When **John Tyler** of Virginia assumed the presidency in April 1841, the nation would again be led by a son of the South. Tyler's predecessor, **William Henry Harrison**, a Virginia native as well, had been elected president in the 1840 contest, but died of pneumonia on April 4, 1841, after serving just one month as ninth US president. Like seven of his forerunners, Tyler was a slaveholder. Moreover, his cabinet appointments confirmed that "slave power"—the belief that a disproportionate share of political power was held by slave owners—controlled the Federal Government.[97]

Portrait of President John Tyler (1790-1862) of Virginia, by American artist George Peter Alexander Healy, 1864. The first vice president to assume the presidency, on the death of President William Henry Harrison, April 4, 1841, Tyler served until March 4, 1845. Image courtesy of the White House Historical Association

During this time, the United States Supreme Court appeared to be part of a slave power triumvirate, as Chief Justice **Roger Taney**, in his opinion in *Prigg v. Pennsylvania* (1842), implied that it was the constitutional duty of all states in the Union to act in accordance with the South.[98] Specifically, the Court ruled that the Federal Government had a responsibility to recover runaway slaves, blunting the efforts of several northern states to offer safety and legal recourse to free blacks.[99]

In 1844, southern Democrats nominated **James Polk** of Tennessee to become president as he was in favor of annexing western territories. Although elected by a narrow margin, Polk orchestrated the largest territorial expansion of the US to date. He succeeded in appropriating Texas in 1845; acquired the Oregon Territory through an 1846 treaty with Britain; and, at the conclusion of America's war with Mexico in 1848, gained control of lands that would become all or part of nine new states through the Treaty of Guadalupe Hidalgo.[100]

Portrait of James K. Polk (1795-1849) of Tennessee by American artist George Peter Alexander Healy, 1846. The eleventh US President, Polk served one term, from 1845 to 1849. Image courtesy of the Smithsonian National Portrait Gallery

The United States was marching ever westward, amassing new territories that would take it all the way to the Pacific Ocean in a quest to create new slave states. Tellingly, each one of these land acquisitions had been spearheaded by a president from a slave state.[101] Now, it was up to white abolitionists, free blacks, and fugitive slaves themselves to inflict the greatest harm slave owners could imagine. Like-minded freedom fighters from Germany would assist in the cause.

A Scientific Challenge to Racism

German anatomist and physiologist **Friedrich Tiedemann** scientifically disproved the basis of racism during the 1830s—a time when the United States was harboring more than two million slaves out of a total population of 12.9 million. A graduate of Marburg University's School of Medicine, Tiedemann in 1836 detailed his research in a lengthy treatise titled *On the Brain of the Negro*, providing an insight into his regard for human rights.[102]

Tiedemann asserted that the African brain is comparable to the Caucasian brain, writing: "As the facts which we have advanced plainly prove that there are no well-marked and essential differences between the brain of the Negro and the European, we must conclude that no innate difference in the intellectual faculties can be admitted to exist between them," adding that the "original and good character of the Negro tribes on the Western Coast of Africa has been corrupted and ruined by the horrors of the slave trade, since they have unfortunately become acquainted with Europeans."[103]

Lithographic portrait of Friedrich Tiedemann (1781-1861), 1835. Image courtesy of the British Museum

On the Brain of the Negro is considered remarkable for its time because it dismissed the deep-rooted Christian argument justifying slavery—that Africans are an inferior race too mentally deficient to govern themselves.[104]

Tiedemann published his treatise in English rather than German because reportedly he wanted to reach an audience in America "where anti-slavery activism had been on the rise since 1830," wrote historian Jeannette Eileen Jones. "Understood in this context," she said, "his article reads as both a scientific treatise and abolitionist tract." Indeed, in 1837 the *Concord Freeman* in Massachusetts cited Tiedemann's treatise in disputing the claims of proslavery activists that Africans are an inferior race.[105]

Chapter Seven

The Forty-Eighters Arrive

"Germany must become a free state like America" read the rallying cry. The sentiment appeared on pamphlets being circulated among the crowd of radicals—insurgents who were cheered by the news that Prussian King **Wilhelm IV**, in March 1848, had agreed to introduce constitutional reforms and unify the German states.[106]

The abdication and forced exile of King **Louis-Philippe** of France just one month earlier and the recent resignation of Prince **Klemens von Metternich** of Austria had proven a European discontent with monarchs out of touch with their people. The German revolutionists, who had eagerly taken to the streets, were heartened that liberal reforms were on the horizon, promising a German republic with liberty and democracy.[107]

In December 1848, however, Wilhelm IV reversed his course by dissolving the newly formed democratic assembly in Berlin, and—regaining his power—directed the army to reoccupy that city. The German Revolution of 1848 had failed. Most of the revolutionists fled Germany to avoid the repercussions of their treason, looking to America as a paragon of national unity. Many viewed the United States as an ideal republic, the American Revolution their source of inspiration.[108]

They came to America as exiles and were called the Forty-Eighters for the year in which they fought for self-government in their homeland. Many turned their liberal passion toward the United States, where, to their utter disappointment, they found its fabric unraveling with the threads of slavery. Their numbers included physicians, jurists, inventors, businessmen, and farmers—all questioning how slave labor could exist in a free society.[109]

Notably, many were journalists who became associated with German-language newspapers that alerted their readers to slavery's inhumanity. In St. Louis, Missouri, **Henry Boernstein** became publisher of the *Anzeiger des Westens* (*Indicator of the West*) in 1851. Also in 1851, **Carl Heinrich Schnauffer** founded *Der Baltimore Wecker* (*The Baltimore Alarm Clock*), and **George Schneider** became editor of the *Illinois Staats-Zeitung* (*Illinois State Newspaper*)—a Chicago newspaper that became influential among German-Americans throughout the entire Midwest. In 1853, **Hermann Raster** became editor of the *New-Yorker Abend Zeitung* (*New York Evening News*).[110]

Friedrich Hecker (1811-1881), with fellow Forty-Eighter Gustav Struve (1805-1870), led what became known as the "Hecker Uprising," an armed rebellion in April 1848 designed to overthrow the government and establish a republic in the Grand Duchy of Baden. Image courtesy of Der Bärenhof, Hinterschollach, Germany

New-Yorker Abend Zeitung,

(The only German Evening Paper,)
Office, 24 North William-street.

Three thousand copies of this paper are published daily, and the circulation is yet increasing, which renders it one of the best and cheapest mediums for advertising. To City subscribers the price is 12 1-2 cents per week, the " ATLANTISCHE BLAETTER," (a Sunday paper.) included. To subscribers in the country the paper is mailed for one year for $6. or $5 exclusive of the Sunday paper. payable in advance.

Advertisement published in 1856 for the German-language newspaper *New-Yorker Abend Zeitung.*

By 1854, eighty-eight German-language newspapers were being published in America, all speaking out against the institution of slavery. During the Civil War years—1861 to 1865—other Forty-Eighters joined the German-language press. These included **Lorenzo Brentano**, editor of the *Illinois Staats-Zeitung*, with **Wilhelm Rapp** as a contributor; **Emil Preetorius**, editor of the *Westliche Post* (*Western Post*) in St. Louis; and **Carl Daenzer**, editor of the *Anzeiger des Westens*, also in St. Louis.[111]

Karl Heinzen, founder of *Der Pionier* (*The Pioneer*) in Louisville, Kentucky, articulated the frustration of his colleagues who had tried but failed to kindle liberty in their homeland: "Opposition to the politics of slavery in America is a battle against reaction in Europe," he wrote. "This republic cannot and will not be able to do anything for European freedom until it has shaken the yoke of slavery from its neck."[112]

The Forty-Eighters also lamented the political power wielded by slave owners in the US, feeling these oppressors were undermining political principles for their own narrow interests. And, believing in national unity as the key to achieving a constitutional government, they worried that the sectionalism wrought by slave owners could result in the Union's collapse.[113]

Considered one of the more radical Forty-Eighters, **Friedrich Kapp** wrote two books on slavery in the years leading up to the Civil War: *The Slavery Question in America* in 1854 and *History of Slavery in the United States* in 1858. During the war, Kapp was a contributing writer to **Caspar Butz**'s scholarly journal *Deutsch-Amerikanische Monatsheft für Politik, Wissenschaft und Literatur* (*German-American Monthly Magazine for Politics, Science and Literature*).[114]

Friedrich Kapp (1824-1884), 1869.

With large German settlements in Fredericksburg and New Braunfels, Texas, at least nine German-language newspapers flourished in that state. One of these was the *San Antonio Zeitung*, founded in 1853 by Forty-Eighter **Carl Adolph Douai**, who had been imprisoned for his role in the German Revolution. Released after one year, he emigrated to America and began publishing the newspaper as an educational and literary tract.[115]

Soon, however, Douai began espousing his abolitionist views, attacking slavery "as an evil incompatible with democratic government." Despite repeated threats of mob violence, Douai continued to press for an end to slavery, even calling for a separate free state in the western part of Texas. Eventually, Douai was forced to sell his interest in the newspaper and moved north, becoming a pioneer of the kindergarten movement.[116]

The most eloquent and well known of the Forty-Eighters was **Carl Schurz**, a student at the University of Bonn during the 1848 Revolution who had enthusiastically joined the radical left. Emigrating to the United States in 1852, Schurz settled in Wisconsin and presented himself as "a spokesman for the many local German-Americans,"[117] viewing slavery as the antithesis of everything he had fought for in Germany.[118]

Recognizing the significance of the German vote—and possessing an extraordinary shrewdness in the art of politics—Schurz was a role model for his countrymen, showing them how to retain their ethnic identity while seeking to become Americans.[119] In the decade ahead, he would bring German immigrants into the party of Lincoln, campaign for the antislavery presidential nominee, and don the uniform of a Union officer, joining his fellow Forty-Eighters in another fight for freedom.

Image of Carl Schurz (1829-1906) published in the German magazine *Die Gartenlaube* (*The Gazebo*) in 1868.

Arriving in America a decade or so before the great controversy between North and South sparked civil war, the Forty-Eighters were able to witness both facets of the slavery question: Is enslaving human beings morally wrong—or essential for the nation's economic health? That these crusaders for liberty chose the path presented to them by the best minds of their German forebears not only revealed their own moral sense, but was an affirmation, as well, of the correct path the Federal Government, at long last, chose to take.

The Forty-Eighter Who Designed an Antislavery Church and School in the Nation's Capitol

A virtual armed encampment during the Civil War (1861-1865), Washington, DC, at war's end looked to men such as Forty-Eighter **Adolf Cluss** to make it into a modern seat of government. By 1900, Cluss had designed or renovated some ninety buildings in the capital city.[120]

Photograph of German-born architect Adolf Cluss (1825-1905), 1900. Image courtesy of the William Shacklette Collection, Smithsonian Institution Castle Collection

His earliest major commission was Calvary Baptist Church at Eighth and H Streets, NW. The founding congregation was comprised of abolitionists who had coalesced four years earlier while the Civil War still raged. At the June 1866 dedication ceremony, the building committee's report was read, stating they had "employed an able architect, who furnished…a beautiful plan, which, with some slight deviation, was matured into the edifice that now stands before you."[121]

Cluss also designed one of the first public schools in the then-segregated Federal City built expressly for African Americans. Completed in 1872, the Charles Sumner School, at 17th and M Streets, NW, was named for the senior senator from Massachusetts. **Charles Sumner** had been a powerful voice against slavery for which he endured a savage beating in 1856 from a proslavery member of the US Senate.[122] The school building was listed on the National Register of Historic Places in 1979.

Photograph of the Adolf Cluss-designed Charles Sumner School, ca. 1890.
The school was renamed the Charles Sumner School Museum and Archives in 1986 and now serves as the District of Columbia's public school repository and museum. Image courtesy of the Charles Sumner School, Washington, DC

Chapter Eight

The Underground Railroad: Routes to Freedom

Perhaps they feared a ruthless overseer or needed to get away from a cruel master. It may have been they were afraid of being handed over to a slave trader, had been beaten too many times, or were anguished because a spouse had been sold South. Or, perhaps they just saw it as a good time to flee.

Whatever the reason, slaves on the run represented an immediate loss to the slave owner—the interruption of work as well as the cost of apprehending or replacing a runaway. Slaves who reached freedom in the North meant an even greater economic loss, for the price of slaves had soared during the 1840s and '50s. Most troubling for slave owners, however, was the recognition that they did not have total control. They regarded a runaway's escape as a personal insult—a challenge to their authority—and paid whatever it cost to have the fugitive captured.[123]

A Ride for Liberty — The Fugitive Slaves, by American artist Eastman Johnson, ca. 1862. Image courtesy of the Brooklyn Museum

When a runaway *was* caught and returned to the plantation, he or she was severely punished as a warning to others who would dare seek freedom. Punitive measures ranged from whipping and shackling in irons to isolation in a cell and even mutilation. And, if a slave master suspected that other slaves knew of a runaway's plans, they might be punished as well.[124]

Still, they ran, knowing they would have to withstand poisonous snakes and numbing cold, and outwit slave patrollers who enjoyed hunting them down. Generally traveling by night, escaping slaves hid in deep forests, tree hollows, corn cribs, haystacks, and caves during the day. To avoid getting lost, fugitive slaves looked for moss growing on the north side of trees and the setting of the sun in the West. With the North Star as a trusted guide, the night skies were a godsend.[125]

For escaping slaves, the night sky played a major role in finding their way to freedom. From the Big Dipper, they could locate the North Star at the end of the handle of the Little Dipper, whose stars are more obscure. German-born astronomer William Herschel (1738-1822), acclaimed for discovering the planet Uranus, was the first, in 1779, to sight the North Star and record its existence.

Among the most likely to escape were slaves living in close proximity to Pennsylvania and Delaware, free states north of the Mason-Dixon Line. Routes from central and western Maryland and northern Virginia led to Pennsylvania, then on to Philadelphia, where a large black community could provide asylum.[126]

Slaves escaping from the Eastern Shore[127] often traveled east through Delaware before venturing north, and those living along the Ohio River in northern Kentucky could look across the water to the free states of Indiana and Ohio, realizing that a raft or boat could carry them to freedom.[128]

It was not unusual, after all, for fugitive slaves to be smuggled onto steamboats plying the Ohio River—or shrouded on sailing vessels heading north from southern ports—as free blacks, abolitionist whites, and former slaves themselves worked to assist runaways in a loosely knit organization called the Underground Railroad.[129]

Photograph of two unidentified escaped slaves, ca. 1861-1865.
Image courtesy of the Library of Congress

Established in the 1830s, the Railroad was not a railroad at all, but rather a collection of benevolent individuals who served as agents, conductors, and station masters—helping fugitive slaves find routes to freedom; furnishing covert transportation in boats and false-bottom wagons; and secreting them from harm in concealed alcoves in homes and churches. Slaves longing for freedom took mental note of the reported trails to follow, which ferrymen could be trusted, and safe places to find food and shelter. Eventually, runaways could find help in every northern state.[130]

Even though the Underground Railroad had no close coordination nor established routes, by 1850 more than a thousand slaves a year were becoming free blacks in the North, most from the border states of Virginia, Maryland, Missouri, and Kentucky. Southern slave owners, who already had intensified their attempts at capture, were of one mind in urging their Congressional representatives to reinforce the original Fugitive Slave Act of 1793, which guaranteed the right of owners to recover escaped slaves and required citizens to assist in their return. Seldom enforced in the North, the existing law was viewed by southerners as largely ineffective.[131]

The Whig Party nominated Zachary Taylor (1784-1850) of Kentucky and Millard Fillmore (1800-1874) of New York to head that party's 1848 presidential ticket. Elected twelfth US President with 47.3 percent of the vote in a three-way race, Taylor (left) was prepared to sign the Compromise of 1850 into law, but died on July 9, 1850. It was thus left to Fillmore to sign the Compromise, which included the Fugitive Slave Act.

The new legislation was the Compromise of 1850, signed by President **Millard Fillmore** on September 18. In addition to admitting California as a free state, the law contained the Fugitive Slave Act of 1850, which met with outrage in the North for its disavowal of basic human rights for runaway slaves. Indeed, the act sided with slave owners in all respects: It denied defendants arrested under its authority the right to a trial by jury, to challenge the legality of their detention, and to testify in their own defense. Further, the Fugitive Slave Act did not allow for exculpatory evidence such as rape or other forms of abuse, required local authorities to assist in recovering absent "human property," and made criminal the humanitarian deed of sheltering a runaway.[132]

Soon after passage, a crush of fugitive slaves fled the United States, fearing the heightened chance they could be returned to slavery. And, as the new law did not make a distinction between those who had been enslaved and those born free, free blacks were terrified of being taken for slaves. Accordingly, 100 black residents of Pittsburgh left for Canada within days of the bill's signing. By the end of September, more than 300 had left the city and the surrounding area—typifying the dread felt by all blacks in the free states.[133]

In response to provisions of the act, black and white abolitionists coalesced to adopt a series of protections. Church bells chimed to disclose the arrival of a suspected slave catcher; homes and churches stepped up their efforts to provide sanctuary; and vigilance committees—which had sprung up in northern cities during the 1830s—intensified their efforts to derail the activities of slave catchers.[134]

In their relentless denunciation of the Fugitive Slave Act, abolitionists routinely publicized the human plight of runaways who were returned to their owners. By doing so, they turned the abstract notion of slavery among those in the North into a reality. In addition, groups of indignant citizens drafted resolutions that castigated the Act as a shameful maneuver that ran counter to the US Constitution.[135]

Just four years after the Fugitive Slave Act of 1850 went into effect, the proslavery-controlled Congress passed a bill that gave way to even greater political turmoil.[136] The Kansas-Nebraska Act, signed by President **Franklin Pierce** on May 30, 1854, repealed the 1820 Missouri Compromise, which had maintained a balance among the states by admitting Missouri as a slave state and Maine, a free state, and which banned slavery from land north of the 36° 30' latitude line.

In addition, the new law created two new territories, Kansas and Nebraska—both north of the 36° 30' parallel—where "popular sovereignty" would reign, meaning the disposition of slavery in the new territories would be left to the will of territorial residents. The Kansas-Nebraska Act thus raised anew the issue of whether slavery should be allowed in the Northwest Territory. To this, antislavery factions reacted bitterly. Seven state legislatures passed resolutions denouncing the repeal of the Missouri Compromise—some pressing for a repeal of the recently signed Fugitive Slave Act. And, between 1855 and 1859, seven states passed personal liberty laws meant to deter slave owners from recovering their human property and prevent the kidnapping of free blacks.[137]

Portrait of Franklin Pierce (1804-1869) of New Hampshire by American artist George Peter Alexander Healy, 1858. Pierce served one term as US president, from 1853 to 1857. Image courtesy of the White House Historical Association

Opposition to the act was particularly formidable in the German-American community. Four months before the bill was signed into law, Forty-Eighter newspaper editors in Pittsburgh hosted a public meeting, declaring: "We are enemies of slavery and consider all extension of it a treason to mankind; adverse to the humanity of the age; adverse to the doctrines of the Declaration of Independence, which taught to all the world that the American people were enlightened and progressive on the subject of human rights."[138]

Eighty out of eighty-eight German-language newspapers came out against the Kansas-Nebraska bill, while Germans living in the border states of Delaware, Maryland, Kentucky, and Missouri began questioning their allegiance to the Democratic Party, whose politicians had championed the measure.[139] Both proslavery and antislavery activists streamed into the Kansas and Nebraska Territories to influence the popular vote.

Slave Hunt, Dismal Swamp, Virginia by British-American painter Thomas Moran, 1862. Located in the Coastal Plain region of southeastern Virginia and northeastern North Carolina, the Great Dismal Swamp served as a refuge for escaping slaves. Image courtesy of the Philbrook Museum of Art, Tulsa, Oklahoma

Keenly aware of the passionate antislavery stance held by German-Americans, **Horace Greeley**, founder and editor of the *New-York Daily Tribune*, wrote: "The Germans are moving all over the North and West. They feel even more deeply than the native citizens."[140]

Reaffirming the Censure of Slavery

At the passage of the 1850 Fugitive Slave Act, world-renowned German explorer and naturalist **Alexander von Humboldt** renewed his criticism of slavery in America, stating: "For 30 years you have not made any progress about slavery. You have gone backward, very far backward in every respect . . . . In Europe you will also find bad things. But I tell you you will not find anything half as bad as your system of slavery, and I know what slavery is like in your country."[141]

Portrait of Alexander von Humboldt (1769-1859) by German artist Joseph
Karl Stieler, 1843. Image courtesy of the Charlottenhof Palace, Prussian
Palaces and Gardens Foundation Berlin-Brandenburg, Germany

Five years earlier, in his masterwork *Kosmos*, Humboldt had also condemned slavery, writing: "In maintaining the unity of the human race we also reject the disagreeable assumption of superior and inferior peoples. Some peoples are more pliable, more highly educated and ennobled by intellectual culture, but there are no races which are more noble than others."[142]

Chapter Nine

Slavery's Westward Expansion

German-language newspapers across the nation, unabashedly partisan in their attitude towards slavery, accomplished much more in the mid-1850s than to point out how the Kansas-Nebraska Act was making a mockery of territorial law. A new political alliance called the Republican Party was formed in March 1854, fewer than three months after the Kansas-Nebraska bill had been introduced on the Senate floor.

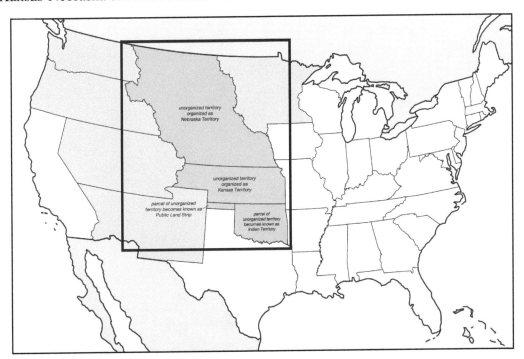

The Kansas-Nebraska Act went into effect on May 30, 1854. The new law created the new territories of Kansas and Nebraska; repealed the Missouri Compromise—which had outlawed slavery above the 36 30' latitude line in the Louisiana Territories— and reopened the national struggle over slavery in the western territories.

Historically, German immigrants to the American colonies and states had aligned themselves with the Democratic Party—the party of **Thomas Jefferson**, writer of the Declaration of Independence; the founding father who symbolized freedom, liberty, and the equality of all men. The Whig Party was founded in 1833 as an alternative, but it was a haven for anti-immigrants and anti-Catholics and so held little appeal to the newly arrived, all of whom were émigrés and a good number Catholic.[143]

Even the Forty-Eighters, more closely allied to the concept of freedom than their immigrant forebears, had favored the Democratic Party. It took just a few short years, however, for them to reevaluate their party allegiance. Clearly, southern slave owners had long identified themselves as Democrats, as did proslavery officials in Washington, DC, whose enmity toward people of African descent was so unbounded that the Federal Government during the 1850s refused passport applications from free black people.[144]

The Kansas-Nebraska bill, passed by the Senate on March 4, 1854, spelled the end of the teetering Whig Party, as the antislavery camp within the party had abandoned its loyalty in favor of coalitions opposed to Kansas-Nebraska. Already weak because of too many factions within, the Whig Party finally disintegrated in the late 1850s.[145]

Photograph of two unidentified border ruffians, ca. 1854-1860.
Image courtesy of the Library of Congress

The Kansas-Nebraska Act had stretched the principle of popular sovereignty into territories that, until now, had outlawed slavery under the Missouri Compromise of 1820. The new measure effectively repealed the earlier compromise, leading antislavery activists to conclude that the Act's defenders wished to extend slavery up and down the hemisphere and guarantee slave owners' hold on the Federal Government.[146]

With settlers allowed to vote whether the Kansas and Nebraska Territories would be admitted to the Union as free states or slave states, activists from both sides of the issue began flooding into the territories to determine the outcome. Support for a new political party was clearly at hand, for Kansas-Nebraska had convinced northerners that a sectional compromise was no longer possible.[147] Meeting in Ripon, Wisconsin, former members of the Whig Party thus founded the Republican Party in opposition to the expansion of slavery. The date was March 20, 1854.

Seeking to bolster participation in the new party, Republican leaders reached out to Forty-Eighter journalists, hoping they would bring fellow Germans into the fold. In response, newspapers such as the *Anzeiger des Westens* (*Indicator of the West*) in St. Louis, Missouri, and the *New-Yorker Demokrat* began publishing articles questioning the ideology of the Democratic Party. **Caspar Butz,** in writing a scathing satire of America's raucous Fourth of July celebrations, described the despicable conditions of slavery and urged fellow Germans not to participate in these galas until all slaves were free.[148]

In addition to the Kansas-Nebraska Act, another staggering blow to abolitionists was Supreme Court Justice **Roger B. Taney**'s ruling in *Dred Scott v. Sandford* (1857). Enslaved in Missouri, **Dred Scott** sued for freedom because his master had taken him to Illinois and Wisconsin Territory, both free, where Scott had lived for several years before returning to the slave state of Missouri. Handing down his landmark decision, Taney ruled that African Americans are not considered citizens under the US Constitution, stating they were "so far inferior that they had no rights which the white man was bound to respect." Taney further ruled that Congress had no authority to forbid slavery in the territories, virtually assuring the expansion of slavery westward.[149]

The Forty-Eighters—some of whom had never committed to a particular party—now proclaimed themselves to be Republicans, motivating other German-Americans, particularly those in the Midwest, to join the party as well. Uniting with the Forty-Eighters were the German revolutionists who had fled to the United States in the 1830s—members of the liberal *Burschenschaft* movement such as **Charles Follen**, **Karl Beck**, and **Gustav Koerner**, who shared the same democratic ideals. They, too, joined the Republican Party and persuaded other German-Americans to follow suit.[150]

Recognizing the importance of the German vote, the Republican Party platform adopted in 1860, in fact, confirmed the attempts made to win the support of German-American voters.[151] In siding primarily with Republicans—and with this, the defeat of slavery—German-Americans had enhanced their ethnic identity as a freedom-loving people.

Portrait of Dred Scott (ca. 1799-1858) painted by German-born artist Louis
Schultze, ca. 1888. Image courtesy of the Missouri History Museum

Portrait of James Buchanan (1791-1868) of Pennsylvania by American artist George Peter Alexander
Healy, 1859. The fifteenth US President, Buchanan was also the last slave-holding president. His one
term in office ran from 1857 to 1861. Image courtesy of the Smithsonian National Portrait Gallery

The Abolitionist Novel That Shook the North

In her famous novel *Uncle Tom's Cabin; or, Life Among the Lowly*, author **Harriet Beecher Stowe** realistically described the wretchedness of slavery, shocking readers in the North and provoking southern slave owners to intensify their defense of the practice.[152]

Portrait of Harriet Beecher Stowe (1811-1896) by American artist Alanson Fisher, 1853. Image courtesy of the Smithsonian National Portrait Gallery

Living in Cincinnati for nearly twenty years, Stowe was able to dramatize the contrast between the free state of Ohio and the slave state of Kentucky. In one of her more memorable passages, the young Eliza escapes "across the Ohio River in the dead of winter," wrote historian Andrew Cayton. "Such were the attractions of Ohio," he said, "that enslaved African Americans would literally jump across ice floes to reach its soil."[153] More than 300,000 copies of the novel were sold in 1852, its first year of publication. In the previous year, the book was serialized in the abolitionist newspaper *The National Era*.

A German translation of *Uncle Tom's Cabin* made Harriet Beecher Stowe Germany's favorite author. So beloved was the writer that a Harriet Beecher Stowe doll was manufactured in Germany ca. 1865.[154]

Chapter Ten

A Bridge to Freedom

Mother Nature was in a blissful frame of mind millions of years ago when she created the Niagara Escarpment. The steep slope, bounded by flat expanses of earth on either side, begins its journey in western New York State, crosses the Niagara River into Ontario, Canada, and then re-enters the United States in Michigan's Upper Peninsula.[155] Its beauty is highlighted at Niagara Falls, where Canada and America share a deep chasm that boasts two magnificent waterfalls.

It was just two kilometers downstream from Niagara Falls that German-American **John Augustus Roebling** designed the first successful railway suspension bridge the world had ever seen. Completed in 1855, his bridge united two nations and unwittingly—although Roebling was indeed antislavery—empowered fleeing slaves from the US to cross safely into Canada.[156]

Built in 1847 to ply the Hudson River, *Armenia* was one of the antebellum steamboats carrying escaped slaves to freedom. Image courtesy of the Great Lakes Maritime Society

Slavery had existed in the region during its territorial days. However, the practice came to an end following passage of the Act Against Slavery in Upper Canada in 1793 and the Slavery

60

Abolition Act in Britain in 1833. While the latter measure did not immediately free Britain's enslaved, the act did stipulate that slaves older than seven would be free after four or six years of apprenticeship. Thus, by 1850, all black residents of Upper Canada had won their freedom.[157]

It was in that year that the southern-controlled US Congress passed, and President **Millard Fillmore** signed, the landmark Fugitive Slave Act, which demanded the seizure and return of freedom seekers running from one of the fifteen southern slave states. While the law outraged abolitionists, it struck sheer terror into the hearts of black people, for it required antislavery citizens to assist slave catchers and provided no redress for free blacks kidnapped and taken as slaves. Canada, long known as the biblical "Canaan" by America's slaves, now truly became the Promised Land.[158]

In earlier decades, slaves escaping into Upper Canada encountered the formidable Great Lakes barriers of Michigan, Erie, and Ontario, as well as the Detroit and Niagara Rivers. Most of the towns along this aqueous border became Underground Railroad terminals, with "conductors" advising fugitive slaves on who could be trusted to carry them across the water on a boat or ferry. Mercifully, most of the ferry captains were understanding, many refusing to charge for the passage.[159]

The slave catcher's role became less burdensome under the Fugitive Slave Law of 1850, which required US citizens to assist in the capture and return of runaway slaves.

Runaway slaves traveling through Pennsylvania or Ohio could reach Buffalo along the Lake Erie shore—from there, crossing the Niagara River by boat to Upper Canada. Lewiston, New York, just twenty-five miles north of Buffalo, maintained a regular ferry service across the Niagara River. Escaping slaves could reach Lewiston on foot, or on steamships that ran daily from Lake Ontario. Youngstown, six miles north of Lewiston, also operated a regular ferry service across the river.[160]

Now, with the Fugitive Slave Act in force, both free and enslaved blacks were fleeing in droves for the safety of Canada, destined, as were their forebears, to cross lakes and rivers to reach the Promised Land. What was needed at Niagara—one of the few places where African Americans could outwit the border—was a bridge.[161]

Two years earlier, in 1848, a Philadelphia architect named **Charles Ellett** had designed a temporary wooden bridge spanning the Niagara River at a site known as Whirlpool Rapids, just north of the Falls. Here the river was at its narrowest, with high cliffs on either side standing only 800 feet apart. The oak-planked bridge, rising 220 feet above the eddying rapids, provided a means for carriages and wagons to take tourists to nearby Niagara Falls. The area had become a mecca for travelers eager to see the spectacular Falls as well as daredevils such as **Charles Blondin**, who thrilled nineteenth-century audiences with an array of fearsome tightrope acts.[162]

Whirlpool Rapids appears at a crook in the Niagara River, masquerading as a maelstrom as it swirls counterclockwise over and around submerged rocks. It was here—at the narrowest part of the river—that John A. Roebling built the "freedom" bridge linking the United States and Canada. Image courtesy of the Library of Congress

While German-born architect John Roebling was completing a bridge over the Monongahela River in Pittsburgh, he received an invitation from the Niagara Falls Suspension Bridge Company to submit plans for a *railway* suspension bridge over the Niagara River—a permanent span at Whirlpool Rapids that could accommodate the weight of a passenger train. Moreover, the new bridge would augment the numerous ferry boats plying the river, which, during the peak summer months, could barely keep up with demand.[163]

Roebling had already proven his genius at bridge-building with his design of two separate spans in Pittsburgh as well as the Lackawaxen Aqueduct in Pennsylvania and the

Delaware Aqueduct. Further, he had come up with the idea of replacing hemp rope with iron-wire roping, and, in 1841, established a wire rope manufacturing plant in Saxonburg, Pennsylvania. With weights attached, and with a wooden frame, swivels, and pulleys, Roebling's rope was more durable than standard wire rope, which had been introduced in the United States in the late 1830s.[164]

Portrait of civil engineer John A. Roebling (1806-1869), ca. 1866-1867. Born in Mühlhausen, Prussia, and educated at the Royal Polytechnic Institute in Berlin, Roebling emigrated to the United States in 1831. Roebling's son, Washington Roebling (1837-1926), served in the Union Army during the Civil War, breveted to colonel at war's end. Image courtesy of the Brooklyn Museum Collection

Roebling began building the Niagara Railway Suspension Bridge in the fall of 1852—his Teutonic qualities of tenaciousness, rigor, and preciseness evident throughout the project. His design called for two levels, an upper trestle for trains and a lower platform for horse-drawn conveyances and pedestrians. When the 825-foot span was opened for traffic in March 1855, it was the first wire-cable suspension bridge that could withstand the weight of a moving locomotive as well as the first to have a stiffened truss that could stand firm against high winds.[165]

Roebling's bridge was said to be "a technical tour de force never again to be repeated."[166] Its value in human terms, however, cannot be overstated. Fugitive slaves on the Underground Railroad crossed the border secreted aboard railroad cars riding Roebling's upper trestle, and traversed the lower level as well on foot or hidden in a wagon or carriage.[167]

A hand-colored lithograph of the Niagara Railway Suspension Bridge in 1856, showing the upper trestle for trains and the lower level for pedestrians and horse-drawn carriages. Niagara Falls can be seen in the background. Image courtesy of the Library of Congress

Though better known for bridge-building, Roebling's deeply felt antislavery sentiments were made apparent in a letter sent in 1832 to his good friend **Frederick Baehr**: "How could an educated German feel happy . . . if he must regard every Negro as a natural enemy, where even the law strictly forbids him to treat the Negro humanely, to educate him, to draw closer to him with kindness, or even to set him free?"[168]

When Roebling's railway suspension bridge was completed in 1855, the daring abolitionist **Harriet Tubman** helped dozens of fugitive slaves[169] over the new bridge, most famously assisting runaway **Joe Bailey** in November 1856: "The cars began to cross the bridge. Harriet was very anxious to have her companions see the Falls . . . . 'Joe, come look at de Falls! Joe, you fool you, come see de Falls! It's your last chance.' But Joe sat still and never raised his head. At length Harriet knew by the rise in the center of the bridge, and the descent on the other side, that they had crossed 'the line.'"[170]

The center of the bridge held particular importance for Harriet Tubman. It was the spot from which runaway slaves could see the rushing Niagara Falls. But the center also meant freedom, for once this line was crossed, no authority operating under the Fugitive Slave Act could wrench them back into slavery.

A carte-de-viste of Harriet Tubman (ca. 1822-1880), 1868. Escaping herself from slavery in Dorchester County, Maryland, Harriet Tubman was known as the "Moses of Her People" for assisting hundreds of slaves to freedom. Image courtesy of the Smithsonian National Museum of African American History and Culture and the Library of Congress

Chapter Eleven

The Struggle for Freedom

John Brown's famous raid at Harper's Ferry, Virginia, and his subsequent hanging was not the match in the powder keg that led to the Civil War, but, to abolitionists, it was the finishing act for proslavery forces who had long made attempts to tilt their notion of democracy toward the South.

Brown had plotted the raid for years, raising money and recruiting both black and white disciples for a planned attack on the national armory in western Virginia. His intention was to strip the arsenal of its guns and ammunition, then march with his men toward the Appalachian Mountains, freeing slaves in open rebellion as they went.[171]

Portrait of abolitionist John Brown (1800-1859) by Norwegian artist Ole Peter Hansen Balling, 1872. Image courtesy of the Smithsonian National Portrait Gallery

During the night of October 16, 1859, Brown and his followers carried out the plan, overrunning the arsenal and taking the night watchman as hostage. Word of the assault spread, however, and, amid a number of casualties, Brown was captured by Federal officers, put on trial in the state of Virginia, and found guilty of treason and murder. In December of that year he was put to death by hanging—thus becoming a martyr for the abolitionist cause.[172]

One of those whose patience with the southern embrace of slavery had reached the breaking point was Forty-Eighter **August Willich**, a featured speaker at an abolitionist meeting held in Cincinnati just two days after Brown's execution. The composition of the audience—about two-thirds German-American and the other one-third of African descent—was reflected in the hall's adornment: the black, red, and gold flag of German republicanism; the red, white, and blue emblem of America; and, on the speaker's platform, a banner bearing the purpose of the meeting, "In Memory of John Brown."[173]

Such German-sponsored rallies so impressed the prominent abolitionist **Frederick Douglass** that he singled out antislavery German-Americans as "the many noble and high-minded men [who] have become our active allies in the struggle against oppression and prejudice."[174]

In *Frederick Douglass Appealing to President Lincoln and His Cabinet to Enlist Negroes*, African American artist William Edouard Scott depicts Frederick Douglass (1818-1895) asking President Lincoln (1809-1865) to bolster his endorsement of African American soldiers. Image courtesy of the Library of Congress

Freedom at Niagara

German-Americans, who began flocking to the Republican Party during the 1850s, now were to play a significant role at the party's 1860 presidential nominating convention, held that May in Chicago. **Carl Schurz** was appointed to the Resolutions Committee and headed the Wisconsin delegation, and **Abraham Lincoln** himself had chosen **Gustav Koerner** to be one of his four at-large delegates. In total, forty-two Germans served as convention delegates, including **Caspar Butz** and **George Schneider** of Illinois, **Hermann Raster** of Ohio, and **Adolph Douai** and **Friedrich Kapp** of New York.[175]

Photograph of Forty-Eighter George Schneider (1823-1905) of Illinois, one of forty-two German-born delegates to the 1860 Republican National Convention. Schneider served as editor of the *Illinois Staats-Zeitung* from 1851 until 1861, at which time President Lincoln appointed him consul general to Denmark.

Schurz had gone into the convention supporting **William H. Seward** of New York, whose condemnation of slavery was indisputable. Schurz, however, switched his allegiance to Lincoln on the second ballot. On the third ballot, it was clear that Lincoln had won. Schurz was selected to be on the committee to present the newly elected candidate with the official announcement of his nomination. Afterward, the Republican National Committee asked Schurz to give speeches in both English and German, principally in German communities. For the rest of the summer and into the fall, Schurz campaigned earnestly for the Republican ticket, contributing to the genial relationship that would develop between him and Lincoln.[176]

Positioned as a foe of slavery in the November contest, Lincoln competed against three other candidates: **John Breckinridge** and **John Bell**, both running on proslavery platforms, and Democrat **Stephen Douglas**, who held that territories should determine the existence of slavery. Although he had won only 39.9 percent of the popular vote, Lincoln triumphed in the Electoral College with a majority of 180 out of 303 votes, carrying all of the free states except New Jersey.[177]

Significantly, Lincoln was rewarded with a majority of the German-American vote, running most impressively among German Protestant voters and German-Americans in the Northwest. Lincoln's victory, however, meant civil war was a certainty, and a succession of eleven southern states opted to leave the Union, beginning with South Carolina on December 20, 1860. Historians have suggested that were it not for the antislavery Germans living in St. Louis and the Lower Missouri River Valley, Missouri would have seceded as well.[178]

When war broke out on April 12, 1861, with the southern bombardment of the Federal garrison at Fort Sumter, South Carolina, German-Americans felt duty bound to enlist. So earnest were these soldiers, the enmity they had for slavery was considered extraordinary as few native-born Union soldiers were so impassioned as they. Indeed, while German-Americans represented roughly 5 percent of the US population, their numbers constituted more than 10 percent of the Union Army.[179]

Moreover, German-American soldiers trained for the military in their home country represented an invaluable component of the Union Army. Particularly adept were German artillery men. It is said that Captain **Hubert Dilger**, born in the Black Forest region and trained at the Karlsruhe Military Academy, was likely the best artilleryman in the Union Army.[180]

Captain Hubert Dilger (1836-1911) was awarded the Medal of Honor for his heroic actions at the Battle of Chancellorsville, Virginia, on May 2, 1863. Image courtesy of the Library of Congress

Until 1864, the Union Army provided for two grades of general officers—brigadier general and major general. Twelve of these generals were German-born: **Louis Blenker, Henry Bohlen, August Kautz, Charles L. Matthies, Peter Joseph Osterhaus, Frederick Salomon, Alexander Schimmelfennig, Carl Schurz, Franz Sigel, Adolph von Steinwehr, Max Weber,** and **August Willich.** Some 200,000 of the two million soldiers who served in the northern army were German-born; about 36,000 of these were in all-German units led by these German commanders.[181]

Brigadier General Peter Joseph Osterhaus (1823-1917), 1863.
Image courtesy of the Missouri History Museum

At the beginning of the war, Steinwehr raised a regiment of German immigrants called the 29th New York Infantry—often referred to as the "First German." Promoted from colonel to brigadier general on July 3, 1862, Steinwehr served in that capacity at both Gettysburg and Chattanooga.[182]

Also early in the war, Sigel accepted a commission as colonel of the 3rd Missouri Infantry, giving him an opportunity to exhibit his ability to recruit German immigrant volunteers. President Lincoln, ever sensitive to the pro-North Forty-Eighters, promoted Sigel to brigadier general in March 1862. Thereafter, "I fights mit Sigel!" became a proud declaration among German-born soldiers.[183]

In the spring of 1862, Lincoln appointed his longtime friend Carl Schurz to the post of brigadier general. Although some looked askance at what they felt was clearly a political appointment, Schulz's demonstrated courage at Second Bull Run in August of that year pacified many doubters.[184]

A pressing issue facing Lincoln during the war was the need for a code of conduct to standardize his officers' actions, particularly with regard to the differing decisions they made regarding the treatment of Confederate prisoners and fugitive slaves seeking refuge. In early 1863, German-born **Franz Lieber** wrote *Instructions for the Government of Armies of the United States Government in the Field,* outlining rules for the conduct of war.[185]

Lincoln distributed the code to his officers in April of that year, providing the needed legal guidance. Throughout the war, Lieber—who had founded the nation's first encyclopedia—was a professor at Columbia University as well as a military advisor for the Union, frequently consulting with Lincoln on issues concerning military and international law.[186]

William Harvey Carney (1840-1908), Medal of Honor recipient, the most decorated African American soldier in the Civil War. Image courtesy of Howard University

On September 22, 1862, Lincoln made an announcement that he would later call "the central act of my administration and the great event of the nineteenth century." It was the Emancipation Proclamation, to become effective January 1, 1863—the momentous document that freed all slaves in the rebel Confederate states, ordered the military to maintain that freedom, and authorized African Americans to join the Union Army and Navy.[187]

A Negro Regiment in Action by German-American illustrator Thomas Nast, published in *Harper's Weekly* on March 14, 1863. Image courtesy of the Metropolitan Museum of Art

   While the Proclamation did not free the nearly half-million slaves in the loyal border states of Delaware, Kentucky, Maryland, Missouri, and West Virginia, the action was met with jubilation among free blacks in the North as well as slaves in the South and runaways who had sought protection from Union forces.[188] Lincoln, henceforth, would be hailed as the "Great Emancipator." Nevertheless, he feared that the Emancipation Proclamation would be scrapped once the war was over, as it was, in effect, a military strategy and not national policy.[189] Realizing that universal emancipation could come about only through a constitutional amendment, Lincoln extended his full support toward the Thirteenth Amendment[190], which read: "Neither slavery nor involuntary servitude, except as a punishment for crime whereof the party shall have been duly convicted, shall exist within the United States, or any place subject to their jurisdiction."

The measure passed in the Senate as early as April 8, 1864, but it did not pass in the House until January 31, 1865. The following day, Lincoln signed a joint resolution asking states to ratify the amendment. Tragically, he died from an assassin's bullet on April 15. Thus, the Great Emancipator did not live to see the Thirteenth Amendment ratified on December 6, 1865.

Scene of the funeral procession for President Abraham Lincoln passing the State House in Columbus, Ohio, April 29, 1865, drawn by German-born cartographer Albert Ruger. Image courtesy of the Library of Congress

Acknowledgments

While I was a history major in college, I was not aware that a German-American had built a bridge in the mid-1800s linking the United States and Canada. It was not until I read Ginger Strand's book, *Inventing Niagara: Beauty, Power, and Lies*, that I learned that runaway slaves from the American South had crossed this bridge to find freedom in Canada.

Then, while researching for my own book, *How German Ingenuity Inspired America*, I learned even more about the German-born bridge builder, John Augustus Roebling — who went on to greater fame with his design of the iconic Brooklyn Bridge. I was intrigued. Had other German-Americans contributed so notably to the abolishment of slavery, America's fatal flaw?

Friends and family members alike were of great assistance as I endeavored to write *Freedom at Niagara* — the story of German-Americans and the roles they played in ridding the United States of this most egregious of institutions.

Valued friends Marilyn Maloney and Brenda Homer sent me numerous articles on the Underground Railroad; treasured family member Jonathon Breen brought little known facts about the Civil War to my attention; and beloved nephew and godson David Simon, with his scholarly knowledge of American history, faithfully reviewed the manuscript before it went to press.

My wonderful husband Earl assisted in countless ways. His vast collection of history books helped tremendously in the research phase, and our trips to the East Coast and to Ontario, Canada, gave life to the historical past. And, certainly, this book would not have been possible without the guidance, knowledge, and support of my cherished friend, Hardy von Auenmueller.

Endnotes

1 "The First Africans," Historic Jamestowne, National Park Service, Department of the Interior, https://historicjamestowne.org/history/the-first-africans/. The English ship, named the *White Lion*, was operating under a Dutch "letter of marque," a license that authorized foreign vessels to participate in the slave-trading business of the Netherlands.

2 Philip D. Morgan, "Virginia Slavery in Atlantic Context, 1550-1650," in *Virginia 1619: Slavery and Freedom in the Making of English America*, ed. Paul Musselwhite, Peter C. Mancall, and James Horn (Williamsburg, VA: Omohundro Institute of Early American History and Culture / Chapel Hill: University of North Carolina Press, 2019), 85, 86; J. David Hacker, "From '20. and Odd' to 10 Million: The Growth of the Slave Population in the United States," National Center for Biotechnology Information, National Library of Medicine, May 13, 2020, https://www.ncbi.nlm.nih.gov/pmc/articles/PMC7716878/.

3 Betty Wood, S*lavery in Colonial America, 1619-1776*, African American History Series (Lanham, MD: Rowman & Littlefield, 2005), 7, 8.

4 Wood, S*lavery in Colonial America*, 9, 10-11.

5 Winthrop D. Jordan, *White Over Black: American Attitudes Toward the Negro, 1550-1812* (Williamsburg, VA: Omohundro Institute of Early American History and Culture / Chapel Hill: University of North Carolina Press, 1968), 73.

6 Harold E. Davis, *The Fledgling Province: Social and Cultural Life in Colonial Georgia, 1733-1776* (Williamsburg, VA: Omohundro Institute of Early American History and Culture / Chapel Hill: University of North Carolina Press, 1976), 125-127. Also known as black codes, slave codes were laws designed to control the behavior of enslaved Africans.

7 Jordan, *White Over Black*, 102-103.

8 Ira Berlin, *Generations of Captivity: A History of African-American Slaves* (Cambridge, MA: Belknap/Harvard University Press, 2003), 82. New Amsterdam was renamed New York in 1664 when it passed from Dutch to English control.

9 Patience Essah, *A House Divided: Slavery and Emancipation in Delaware, 1638-1865* (Charlottesville: University Press of Virginia, 1996), 2; Jordan, *White Over Black*, 103.

10 David Hackett Fischer, *Albion's Seed: Four British Folkways in America* (New York: Oxford University Press, 1991), 52-53. The growing season in New England ran from late May to early October, two months shorter than in the Chesapeake region. In addition, the harsh temperatures during the winter months proved to be perilous for immigrants from tropical Africa.

11 Marc Howard Ross, *Slavery in the North: Forgetting History and Recovering Memory* (Philadelphia: University of Pennsylvania Press, 2018), 4, 5.

12 Jordan, *White Over Black*, 103; William D. Pierson, *Black Yankees: The Development of an Afro-American Subculture in Eighteenth-Century New England* (Amherst: University of Massachusetts Press, 1988), 42-43.

13 Hacker, "From '20. and Odd.'"

14 Ingrid Schöberl, "Franz Daniel Pastorius and the Foundation of Germantown," in *Germans to America: 300 Years of Immigration, 1683 to 1983*, ed. Günter Moltmann, trans. Robert W. Culverhouse (Stuttgart, DEU: Institute for Foreign Cultural Relations, 1982), 17, 18, 19, 21; "Germantown Quaker Petition Against Slavery," National Park Service, Department of the Interior, https://www.nps.gov/articles/quakerpetition.htm. The revered German artist Albert Dürer in 1521 painted one of the earliest portraits of an African in Europe. Twenty years old, Catherine was a servant to Joanno Brando, a Portuguese trader. See Hans W. Debrunner, "Africa, Europe, and America: The Modern Roots from a European Perspective," in *Crosscurrents: African Americans, Africa, and Germany in the Modern World*, ed. David McBride, Leroy Hopkins, and C. Aisha Blackshire-Belay (Columbia, SC: Camden House, 1998), 8.

15 The concept of the divine spark is the belief that every human being has a connection to God.

16 Julia Jorati, "Leibniz on Slavery and the Ownership of Human Beings," *Journal of Modern Philosophy* 1, no. 1 (December 4, 2019), https://jmphil.org/articles/10.32881/jomp.45/.

17 John H. Zammito, "Policing Polygeneticism in Germany, 1775 (Kames), Kant, and Blumenbach," in *The German Invention of Race*, ed. Sara Eigen and Mark Larrimore, SUNY Philosophy and Race Series (Albany: State University of New York Press, 2006), 43, 47.

18 Johann Friedrich Blumenbach, *On the Natural Varieties of Mankind* (New York: Bergman, 1969), 303.

19 Jeff Broadwater, *James Madison: A Son of Virginia & a Founder of the Nation* (Chapel Hill: University of North Carolina Press, 2012), 187-188.

20 By 1776, between 70,000 and 100,000 German immigrants had settled in the colonies, a number of whom participated in the Revolutionary War. Among these were Major General Friedrich Wilhelm von Steuben (1730-1794), who reorganized the Continental Army; Brigadier General Nicholas Herkimer (ca. 1728-1777), mortally wounded at the Battle of Oriskany; and Major General Johann de Kalb (1721-1780), who lost his life at the Battle of Camden. See Klaus Wust and Heinz Moos, eds., *Three Hundred Years of German Immigrants in North America, 1683-1983: Their Contributions to the Evolution of the New World* (Munich, DEU: Heinz Moos, 1983), 7.

21 Henry F. May, *The Enlightenment in America* (New York: Oxford University Press, 1976), 133.

22 Robert G. Parkinson, *Thirteen Clocks: How Race United the Colonies and Made the Declaration of Independence* (Williamsburg, VA: Omohundro Institute of Early American History and Culture / Chapel Hill: University of North Carolina Press, 2021), 85, 161.

23 Ira Berlin, "Coming to Terms with Slavery in Twenty-First Century America," in *Slavery and Public History: The Tough Stuff of American Memory*, ed. James Oliver Horton and Lois E. Horton (Chapel Hill: University of North Carolina Press, 2009), 2.

24 The Continental Congress served as the governing body of the American colonies prior to the nation's independence.

25 Patrick Rael, *Eighty-Eight Years: The Long Death of Slavery in the United States, 1777-1865*, Race in the Atlantic World, 1700-1900 Series (Athens: University of Georgia Press, 2015), 73; Parkinson, *Thirteen Clocks*, 51.

26 Jean R Soderlund, *Quakers and Slavery: A Divided Spirit* (Princeton, NJ: Princeton University Press, 1985), 4, 12, 139, 171, 173, 185.

27 Marc Howard Ross, *Slavery in the North: Forgetting History and Recovering Memory* (Philadelphia: University of Pennsylvania Press, 2018), 56, 72.

28 Richard Brookhiser, *Give Me Liberty: A History of America's Exceptional Idea* (New York: Basic Books, 2019), 102. It was not until 1804 that New Jersey passed a gradual emancipation act. New York State completely abolished slavery in 1827.

29 Rhode Island was the only state that did not send delegates. Of the 55 delegates, about 25 owned slaves. See Steven Mintz, "Historical Context: The Constitution and Slavery," History Resources, Gilder Lehrman Institute of American History, https://www.gilderlehrman.org/history-resources/teaching-resource/historical-context-constitution-and-slavery.

30 The term "slave" did not appear in the US Constitution until the Thirteenth Amendment was ratified in 1865.

31 Paul Finkelman, *Slavery and the Founders: Race and Liberty in the Age of Jefferson* (Armonk, NY: M.E. Sharpe, 1996), 4.

32 Mintz, "Historical Context." Mintz points out that Thomas Jefferson would have lost the presidential election of 1800 if the Three-Fifths Compromise had not been in effect.

33 Rael, *Eighty-Eight Years*, 73; Finkelman, *Slavery and the Founders*, 6.

34 Horst Dippel, *Germany and the American Revolution, 1770-1800: A Sociohistorical Investigation of Late Eighteenth-Century Political Thinking*, trans. Bernhard A. Uhlendorf (Williamsburg, VA: Omohundro Institute of Early American History and Culture / Chapel Hill: University of North Carolina Press, 1977), 201. With few exceptions, German-born farmers in New England, Pennsylvania, Virginia, Missouri, Texas, and throughout the Deep South neither owned slaves nor approved of the practice. See Kristen Layne Anderson, *Abolitionizing Missouri: German Immigrants and Racial Ideology in Nineteenth-Century America*, Antislavery, Abolition, and the Atlantic World Series (Baton Rouge: Louisiana State University Press, 2016), 3; A. Glenn Crothers, *Quakers Living in the Lion's Mouth: The Society of Friends in Northern Virginia, 1730-1865* (Gainesville: University Press of Florida, 2012), 229; Karolyn Smardz Frost, *I've Got a Home in Glory Land: A Lost Tale of the Underground Railroad* (New York: Farrar, Straus and Giroux, 2008), 119; James Marten, *Texas Divided: Loyalty and Dissent in the Lone Star State, 1856-1874* (Lexington: University Press of Kentucky, 1990), 27, 106, 107; Robert Secor, ed., *Pennsylvania 1776* (University Park: Pennsylvania State University Press, 1976), 122; Colin Woodard, *American Nations: A History of the Eleven Rival Regional Cultures of North America* (New York: Penguin, 2012), 96-97.

35 Five states—Ohio (1803), Indiana (1816), Illinois (1818), Michigan (1837), and Wisconsin (1848)—were created from the Northwest Territory. See Finkelman, *Slavery and the Founders*, 34.

36 Paul Finkelman, "Slavery and Bondage in the 'Empire of Liberty,'" in *Northwest Ordinance: Essays on Its Formulation, Provisions, and, Legacy*, ed. Frederick D. Williams (East Lansing: Michigan State University Press, 1989), 62, 63-64, 66.

37 Gail Collins, *William Henry Harrison*, American Presidents Series (New York: Henry Holt, 2012), 26, 33.

38 Laura Dassow Walls, *The Passage to Cosmos: Alexander von Humboldt and the Shaping of America* (Chicago, IL: University of Chicago Press, 2009), 26.

39 Eleanor Jones Harvey, "Who Was Alexander von Humboldt?" *Smithsonian Magazine*, March 24, 2020, https://www.smithsonianmag.com/smithsonian-institution/who-was-alexander-von-humboldt-180974473/. Humboldt was so passionate in his loathing of slavery that he persuaded the King of Prussia in 1857 to pro-

claim that any slave would become free upon entering Prussia, even though slavery did not exist in the German state. See Philip S. Foner, "Alexander von Humboldt on Slavery in America," *Science & Society* 47, no. 3 (fall 1983), https://www.jstor.org/stable/40402500.

40 Walls, *Passage to Cosmos*, 107, 145-147, 173.

41 In 1800, there were a reported 908,036 enslaved persons in the United States; on the eve of the Civil War (1860), a reported 3,953,760. See J. David Hacker, "From '20. and Odd' to 10 Million: The Growth of the Slave Population in the United States," National Center for Biotechnology Information, National Library of Medicine, May 13, 2020, https://www.ncbi.nlm.nih.gov/pmc/articles/PMC7716878/.

42 Kenneth M. Stampp, *The Peculiar Institution: Slavery in the Ante-Bellum South* (New York: Knopf, 1956), 27; James Walvin, *Freedom: The Overthrow of the Slave Empires* (London, UK: Robinson, 2019), 46, 48.

43 Edward E. Baptist, *The Half Has Never Been Told: Slavery and the Making of American Capitalism* (New York: Basic Books, 2014), 82, 116; Walvin, *Freedom*, 45.

44 Eugene D. Genovese, *Roll, Jordan, Roll: The World the Slaves Made* (New York: Pantheon, 1974), 5; Deborah Gray White, "Simple Truths: Antebellum Slavery in Black and White," in *Passages to Freedom: The Underground Railroad in History and Memory*, ed. David W. Blight (Washington, DC: Smithsonian / New York: Collins, 2006), 44.

45 Tom Lewis, *Washington: A History of Our National City* (New York: Basic Books, 2015), 128; Ira Berlin, *Slaves Without Masters: The Free Negro in the Antebellum South* (New York: New Press, 1974), 15, 16, 20.

46 Carol Wilson, *Freedom at Risk: The Kidnapping of Free Blacks in America, 1780-1865* (Lexington: University Press of Kentucky, 1994), 1, 9-11.

47 White, "Simple Truths," 34, 35. During harvest time, slaves were expected to work eighteen-hour days.

48 White, "Simple Truths," 35-36.

49 White, "Simple Truths," 42.

50 Harriet Jacobs, *Incidents in the Life of a Slave Girl: Written by Herself* (New York: Barnes & Noble Classics, 2005), 85-86.

51 Walvin, *Freedom*, 48.

52 Genovese, *Roll, Jordan, Roll*, 14.

53 White, "Simple Truths," 40; Genovese, *Roll, Jordan, Roll*, 42-43; Velma Maia Thomas, *Lest We Forget: The Passage from Africa into the Twenty-First Century* (Bellevue, WA: Becker & Mayer, 2018), 25.

54 White, "Simple Truths," 41, 42. In the southern slave states, "every white man and woman [had] power over every black man and woman."

55 White, "Simple Truths," 56; John Hope Franklin and Loren Schweninger, *Runaway Slaves: Rebels on the Plantation* (New York: Oxford University Press, 1999), 2; Ralph Young, *Dissent: The History of an American Idea* (New York: New York University Press, 2015), 115.

56 Stampp, *Peculiar Institution*, 118; Franklin and Schweninger, *Runaway Slaves*, 23.

57 Genovese, *Roll, Jordan, Roll*, 9, 10; Walvin, *Freedom*, 61.

58 "Missouri Compromise Ushers in New Era for the Senate," United States Senate, Historical Highlights, https://www.senate.gov/artandhistory/history/minute/Missouri_Compromise.htm.

59 "Missouri Compromise."

60 Thomas S. Hansen, "Charles Follen: Brief Life of a Vigorous Reformer: 1796-1840," *Harvard Magazine*, September-October 2002, https://www.harvardmagazine.com/2002/09/charles-follen.html.

61 Lina Mann, "Building the White House," Slavery in the President's Neighborhood, White House Historical Association, January 3, 2020, https://www.whitehousehistory.org/building-the-white-house. More than 400 slaves helped build the Capitol. See Jesse J. Holland, *Black Men Built the Capitol: Discovering African-American History In and Around Washington, D.C.* (Guilford, CT: Lyons, 2007), 3, 4.

62 Chris Myers Asch and George Derek Musgrove, *Chocolate City: A History of Race and Democracy in the Nation's Capital* (Chapel Hill: University of North Carolina Press, 2017), 20. In early 2023, the Lorton, Virginia, church where President Washington prayed honored the enslaved laborers who helped build the house of worship. Two commemorative plaques were placed inside Pohick Episcopalian Church and dedicated in a special ceremony in March of that year. Washington had been one of the benefactors who financially supported the building of the church, completed in 1774. See Dave Kindy, "Va. Church Where George Washington Prays Honors Its Enslaved Builders," *The Washington Post*, March 15, 2023, https://www.washingtonpost.com/history/2023/03/15/pohick-church-george-washington-enslaved/.

63 Asch and Musgrove, Chocolate City, 23, 24.

64 Asch and Musgrove, *Chocolate City*, 24, 25; Tom Lewis, *Washington: A History of Our National City* (New York: Basic Books, 2015), 6. In 1847, the portion of Washington, DC, that had originally belonged to Virginia was retroceded. Thus, Maryland became the only state to provide land for the Federal City.

65 Asch and Musgrove, *Chocolate City*, 34, 39, 45. The Organic Act of 1801 granted Congress control over the District of Columbia. See 36-37.

66 Nathaniel Philbrick, *Travels with George: In Search of Washington and His Legacy* (New York: Viking, 2021), 290-291.

67 Philbrick, T*ravels with George*, 291.

68 Philbrick, *Travels with George*, 291.

69 Lewis, *Washington*, 83.

70 Lewis, *Washington*, 83.

71 Lewis, *Washington*, 69; Adam Costanzo, *George Washington's Washington: Visions for the National Capital in the Early American Republic*, Early American Places Series (Athens: University of Georgia Press, 2018), 53; Damani Davis, "Slavery and Emancipation in the Nation's Capital," *Prologue Magazine* 42, no. 1 (spring 2010), National Archives, https://www.archives.gov/publications/prologue/2010/spring/dcslavery.html. Washington retained its southern character throughout the Antebellum Period by allowing slavery to flourish. The practice did not end in the nation's capital until April 16, 1862, when President Lincoln signed the Compensated Emancipation Act. It was the only time such a measure had been enacted by any city or state during the Civil War. See "Landmark Legislation: The District of Columbia Compensated Emancipation Act," United States Senate, https://www.senate.gov/artandhistory/history/common/generic/DCEmancipationAct.htm.

72 Holland, *Black Men Built the Capitol*, 26.

73 Jeff Forret, "The Notorious 'Yellow House' That Made Washington, D.C. a Slavery Capital," *Smithsonian Magazine*, July 22, 2020, https://www.smithsonianmag.com/history/how-yellow-house-helped-make-washington-dc-slavery-capital-180975378/.

74 Forret, "Notorious 'Yellow House.'"

75 Holland, *Black Men Built the Capitol*, 28; Asch and Musgrove, *Chocolate City*, 70-71.

76 Edwin Emery, *The Press and America: An Interpretative History of the Mass Media*, 3rd ed. (Englewood Cliffs, NJ: Prentice-Hall, 1972), 57-64.

77 Jon Meacham, *American Lion: Andrew Jackson in the White House* (New York: Random House, 2008), 304, 305.

78 Linda Bramble, *Black Fugitive Slaves in Early Canada*, Vanwell History Project Series (St. Catharines, ON: Vanwell, 1988), 19-20.

79 Natasha L. Henry, *Emancipation Day: Celebrating Freedom in Canada* (Toronto, ON: Dundurn, 2010), 18, 37; Michael Power, "Simcoe and Slavery," in *Slavery and Freedom in Niagara*, ed. Michael Power and Nancy Butler, with Joy Ormsby (Niagara-on-the-Lake, ON: Niagara Historical Society, 2012), 12.

80 John N. Jackson, *The Mighty Niagara: One River—Two Frontiers*, with John Burtniak and Gregory P. Stein (Amherst, NY: Prometheus, 2003), 99, 101; Robin W. Winks, *Canada and the United States: The Civil War Years* (Baltimore: Johns Hopkins University Press, 1960), 3.

81 Power, "Simcoe and Slavery," 24.

82 Henry, *Emancipation Day*, 41-42.

83 Henry, *Emancipation Day*, 41-42. Upper Canada was the first British colony to prohibit the importation of slaves.

84 Robin W. Winks, *The Blacks in Canada: A History*, 2nd ed. (Montréal, QC: McGill-Queen's University Press, 2008), 47, 50, 51.

85 Daniel G. Hill, *The Freedom-Seekers: Blacks in Early Canada* (Agincourt, ON: Book Society of Canada Limited, 1981), 18; Peter C. Newman, *Hostages to Fortune: The United Empire Loyalists and the Making of Canada* (Toronto: ON: Simon & Schuster Canada, 2016), 151; Mary Beacock Fryer and Christopher Dracott, *John Graves Simcoe, 1752-1806: A Biography* (Toronto, ON: Dundurn, 1998), 112.

86 Eric Metaxas, *Amazing Grace: William Wilberforce and the Heroic Campaign to End Slavery* (New York: HarperOne, 2008), 112, 205, 211.

87 Henry, *Emancipation Day*, 42.

88 Thomas F. Gossett, *Race: The History of an Idea in America*, 2nd ed. (New York: Oxford University Press, 1997), 87. The Teutons were an ancient people who spoke a language of the Germanic branch of the Indo-European language family. The favorable term is often used in reference to the people of Germany.

89 Ted Widmer, *Martin Van Buren*, American Presidents Series (New York: Henry Holt, 2005), 110.

90 Ronald L. Heinemann, John G. Kolp, Anthony S. Parent, Jr., and William G. Shade, *Old Dominion, New Commonwealth: A History of Virginia, 1607-2007* (Charlottesville: University of Virginia Press, 2007), 174-175. Earlier slave insurrections had taken place in South Carolina (1739), New York City (1741), Virginia (1800), and Louisiana (1811). See Henry Louis Gates, Jr., "Did African-American Slaves Rebel?" The African Americans: Many Rivers to Cross, Public Broadcasting Service, https://www.pbs.org/wnet/african-americans-many-rivers-to-cross/history/did-african-american-slaves-rebel/.

91 Jenny Bourne, "Slavery in the United States," *EH.Net Encyclopedia*, Economic History Association,

March 26, 2008, https://eh.net/encyclopedia/slavery-in-the-united-states/; James Walvin, *Freedom: The Overthrow of the Slave Empires* (London, UK: Robinson, 2019), 51.

92 Eugene D. Genovese, *Roll, Jordan, Roll: The World the Slaves Made* (New York: Pantheon, 1974), 561, 562; Stephanie M.H. Camp, *Closer to Freedom: Enslaved Women and Everyday Resistance in the Plantation South,* Gender and American Culture Series (Chapel Hill: University of North Carolina Press, 2004), 107.

93 Martha J. Cutter, *The Illustrative Slave: Empathy, Graphic Narrative, and the Visual Culture of the Transatlantic Abolition Movement, 1800-1852* (Athens: University of Georgia Press, 2017), 139; Henry Mayer, *All on Fire: William Lloyd Garrison and the Abolition of Slavery* (New York: Norton, 2008), 109, 110, 112.

94 Joanne B. Freeman, *The Field of Blood: Violence in Congress and the Road to Civil War* (New York: Farrar, Straus and Giroux, 2018), 112; Jack Kelly, *Heaven's Ditch: God, Gold, and Murder on the Erie Canal* (New York: St. Martin's, 2016), 242, 243.

95 Freeman, *Field of Blood*, 5, 113. The gag rules were in effect between 1836 and 1844.

96 Widmer, *Martin Van Buren*, 113.

97 Edward P. Crapol, *John Tyler: The Accidental President* (Chapel Hill: University of North Carolina Press, 2006), 68.

98 Thomas D. Morris, *Southern Slavery and the Law, 1619-1860*, Studies in Legal History Series (Chapel Hill: University of North Carolina Press, 1996), 340.

99 David Brion Davis, *Inhuman Bondage: The Rise and Fall of Slavery in the New World* (New York: Oxford University Press, 2006), 265.

100 "The Annexation of Texas, the Mexican-American War, and the Treaty of Guadalupe-Hidalgo, 1845-1848," Office of the Historian, Department of State, https://history.state.gov/milestones/1830-1860/texas-annexation. By the terms of the Treaty of Guadalupe Hidalgo, officially ending the Mexican-American War (1846-1848), the United States acquired territory that would form the present-day states of California, Nevada, Utah, and New Mexico, most of Arizona and Colorado, and parts of Oklahoma, Kansas, and Wyoming.

101 Kevin Waite, *West of Slavery: The Southern Dream of a Transcontinental Empire*, David J. Weber Series in the New Borderlands History (Chapel Hill: University of North Carolina Press, 2021), 14.

102 J. David Hacker, "From '20. and Odd' to 10 Million: The Growth of the Slave Population in the United States," National Center for Biotechnology Information, National Library of Medicine, May 13, 2020, https://www.ncbi.nlm.nih.gov/pmc/articles/PMC7716878/; "Friedrich Tiedemann (1781-1861)," Universität Heidelberg, University Library, https://www.ub.uni-heidelberg.de/Englisch/helios/digi/anatomie/tiedemann.html.

103 Stephen Jay Gould, "The Great Physiologist of Heidelberg—Friedrich Tiedemann—Brief Article," *Natural History*, July 1999, http://laboratoriogene.info/Ciencia_Hoje/Physiologist_Heidelberg.pdf.

104 Gould, "The Great Physiologist."

105 Jeannette Eileen Jones, "On the Brain of the Negro: Race, Abolitionism, and Friedrich Tiedemann's Scientific Discourse on the African Diaspora," in *Germany and the Black Diaspora: Points of Contact, 1250-1914*, ed. Mischa Honeck, Martin Klimke, and Anne Kuhlmann (New York: Berghahn, 2013), 135, 136, 147.

106 Mischa Honeck, *We Are the Revolutionists: German-Speaking Immigrants and American Abolitionists After 1848*, Race in the Atlantic World, 1700-1900 Series (Athens: University of Georgia Press, 2011), 13, 14. The German Confederation (*Deutscher Bund*) existed at this time. Created in 1815, it consisted of thirty-nine predominately German-speaking sovereign states in Central Europe.

107 Honeck, *Revolutionists*, 13, 14.

108 James J. Sheehan, *Germany History, 1770-1866*, Oxford History of Modern Europe Series (Oxford, UK: Clarendon, 1993), 704-705; Carl Wittke, *Refugees of Revolution: The German-Forty-Eighters in America* (Westport, CT: Greenwood, 1970), v; Honeck, *Revolutionists*, 14, 15.

109 Donald Allendorf, *Your Friend, As Ever: A. Lincoln: How the Unlikely Friendship of Gustav Koerner and Abraham Lincoln Changed America* (Gretna, LA: Pelican, 2014), 147; Wittke, *Refugees of Revolution*, v, 192.

110 Carl Wittke, *The German-Language Press in America* (Lexington: University of Kentucky Press, 1957), 85, 93, 94, 95; "*Illinois Staats-Zeitung*," Academic Dictionaries and Encyclopedias, https://en-academic.com/dic.nsf/enwiki/11528635.

111 Steven Rowan, "Emil Preetorius (1827-1905)," *Missouri Encyclopedia*, https://missouriencyclopedia.org/people/preetorius-emil; Wittke, *German-Language Press*, 96.

112 James M. Bergquist, "The Forty-Eighters: Catalysts of German-American Politics," in *The German-American Encounter: Conflict and Cooperation Between Two Cultures, 1800-2000*, ed. Frank Trommler and Elliott Shore (New York: Berghahn, 2001), 23.

113 Kristen Layne Anderson, *Abolitionizing Missouri: German Immigrants and Racial Ideology in Nineteenth-Century America*, Antislavery, Abolition, and the Atlantic World Series (Baton Rouge: Louisiana State University Press, 2016), 31.

114 "Friedrich Kapp," *The Nation* 39, no. 1010 (November 6, 1884), https://en.wikisource.org/wiki/Friedrich_Kapp; Wittke, *German-Language Press*, 100-101, 189; Bruce Levine, *The Spirit of 1848: German Immigrants, Labor Conflict, and the Coming of the Civil War* (Urbana: University of Illinois Press, 1992), 149.

115 Wittke, *German-Language Press*, 100-101, Marilyn M. Sibley, "Douai, Carl Daniel Adolph, (1819-1888)," *Handbook of Texas*, Texas State Historical Association, https://www.tshaonline.org/handbook/entries/douai-carl-daniel-adolph. Approximately 11,000 Germans settled in West Texas during the 1850s. See Wittke, *Refugees of Revolution*, 193.

116 Sibley, "Douai, Carl Daniel Adolph."

117 Hans L. Trefousse, "Abraham Lincoln and Carl Schurz," in *The German Forty-Eighters in the United States*, ed. Charlotte L. Brancaforte (New York: Peter Lang, 1989), 179, 180.

118 Alison Clark Efford, *German Immigrants, Race, and Citizenship in the Civil War Era* (New York: Cambridge University Press, 2014), 53-54. Efford notes that German-Americans "celebrated ethnic pluralism, not white supremacy, in their popular culture." Accordingly, few German immigrants attended minstrel shows, known for their racist theatrical entertainment. Further, German-language newspapers did not carry advertisements for minstrel shows. See Efford, 76.

119 Trefousse, "Abraham Lincoln and Carl Schurz," 182-183.

120 "Adolf Cluss As the Dominant Architect for the Red Brick City," https://www.adolf-cluss.org/index.php?sub=3.5&content=w&lang=en.

121 "8th and H Streets NW - The Calvary Baptist Church," Streets of Washington, July 20, 2010, http://www.streetsofwashington.com/2010/07/8th-and-h-streets-nw-calvary-baptist.html.

122 "Adolf Cluss Buildings: Sumner School," https://www.adolf-cluss.org/index.php?lang=en&topSub=washington&content=h&sub=3.5.59; "The Caning of Senator Charles Sumner," United States Senate, Historical Highlights, https://www.senate.gov/artandhistory/history/minute/The_Caning_of_Senator_Charles_Sumner.htm.

123 Velma Maia Thomas, *Lest We Forget: The Passage from Africa into the Twenty-First Century* (Bellevue, WA: Becker & Mayer, 2018), 26; David Brion Davis, *The Problem of Slavery in the Age of Emancipation* (New York: Knopf, 2014), 237; James Walvin, *Freedom: The Overthrow of the Slave Empires* (London, UK: Robinson, 2019), 58. Escaping female slaves were considered a greater loss than runaway men because women in their child-bearing years had the potential of producing the next generation of slaves. See Karolyn Smardz Frost, *I've Got a Home in Glory Land: A Lost Tale of the Underground Railroad* (New York: Farrar, Straus and Giroux, 2008), 208-209.

124 Thomas, *Lest We Forget*, 27.

125 Deborah Gray White, "Simple Truths: Antebellum Slavery in Black and White," in *Passages to Freedom: The Underground Railroad in History and Memory*, ed. David W. Blight (Washington, DC: Smithsonian / New York: Collins, 2006), 58; Thomas, *Lest We Forget*, 27; Cheryl Janifer LaRoche, *Free Black Communities and the Underground Railroad: The Geography of Resistanc*e (Urbana: University of Illinois Press, 2014), 88, 89, 90.

126 John Hope Franklin and Loren Schweninger, *Runaway Slaves: Rebels on the Plantation* (New York: Oxford University Press, 1999), 25; R.J.M. Blackett, *The Captive's Quest for Freedom: Fugitive Slaves, the 1850 Fugitive Slave Law, and the Politics of Slavery*, Slavery Since Emancipation Series (New York: Cambridge University Press, 2018), 313.

127 The Eastern Shore is also known as the Delmarva Peninsula. This 170-mile-long land area encompasses nearly all of the state of Delaware as well as the easternmost counties of Maryland and Virginia. The Chesapeake Bay is the Peninsula's western boundary; the Atlantic Ocean, its eastern boundary. The word "Delmarva" is derived from letters in the names of the three states.

128 Blackett, *Captive's Quest for Freedom*, 313; Keith P. Griffler, *Front Line of Freedom: African Americans and the Forging of the Underground Railroad in the Ohio Valley*, Ohio River Valley Series (Lexington: University Press of Kentucky, 2004), 2; Frost, *Home in Glory Land*, 120. Because of the great distance to a free state, fugitive slaves from the Deep South rarely made a successful escape. See Fergus M. Bordewich, *Bound for Canaan: The Underground Railroad and the War for the Soul of America* (New York: Amistad, 2005), 115.

129 Walvin, *Freedom*, 153, 154. With numerous free blacks working on ships, escaping slaves using water transportation could depend on these seamen to be "willing accomplices." See John Michael Vlach, "Above Ground on the Underground Railroad: Places of Flight and Refuge," in *Passages to Freedom: The Underground Railroad in History and Memory*, ed. David W. Blight (Washington, DC: Smithsonian / New York: Collins, 2006), 104.

130 Eric Foner, *Gateway to Freedom: The Hidden History of the Underground Railroad* (New York: Norton, 2015), 18-19; Griffler, *Front Line of Freedom*, 101; Franklin and Schweninger, *Runaway Slaves*,116; LaRoche, *Free Black Communities*, 1-3, 89; Vlach, "Above Ground," 96; Patrick Rael, *Eighty-Eight Years: The Long Death of Slavery in the United States, 1777-1865*, Race in the Atlantic World, 1700-1900 Series (Athens: University of Georgia Press, 2015), 205.

131 Andrew Delbanco, *The War Before the War: Fugitive Slaves and the Struggle for America's Soul from the Revolution to the Civil War* (New York: Penguin, 2018), 36; Walvin, *Freedom*, 155, 156; Stanley W. Campbell, *The Slave Catchers: Enforcement of the Fugitive Slave Law, 1850-1860*, 2nd ed. (Chapel Hill: University of North Carolina Press, 1970), 6, 8, 9, 15.

132 R.J.M. Blackett, "'Freemen to the Rescue!': Resistance to the Fugitive Slave Law of 1850," in *Passages to Freedom: The Underground Railroad in History and Memory*, ed. David W. Blight (Washington, DC: Smithsonian / New York: Collins, 2006), 134-135; Walvin, *Freedom*, 156; Delbanco, *War Before the War*, 5.

133 Blackett, "Freemen to the Rescue!," 137; Walvin, *Freedom*, 156.

134 Blackett, "Freemen to the Rescue!," 139-141.

135 Martha J. Cutter, *The Illustrative Slave: Empathy, Graphic Narrative, and the Visual Culture of the Transatlantic Abolition Movement, 1800-1852* (Athens: University of Georgia Press, 2017), 139; Henry Mayer, *All on Fire: William Lloyd Garrison and the Abolition of Slavery* (New York: Norton, 2008), 109-112; Campbell, *Slave Catchers*, 51.

136 William E. Gienapp, *The Origins of the Republican Party, 1852-1856* (New York: Oxford University Press, 1987), 81

137 Campbell, *Slave Catchers*, 81, 86.

138 Bruce Levine, *The Spirit of 1848: German Immigrants, Labor Conflict, and the Coming of the Civil War* (Urbana: University of Illinois Press, 1992), 154.

139 Albert Bernhardt Faust, *The German Element in the United States,* Vol. II: *The Influence of the German Element in the United States* (New York: Arno Press and *The New York Times*, 1969), 129-130, 131.

140 Levine, *Spirit of 1848*, 156.

141 Hartmut Keil, "Race and Ethnicity: Slavery and the German Radical Tradition," Presentation given in Madison, Wisconsin, February 3, 1999, sponsored by the Max Kade Institute for German-American Studies and the Center for the History of Print Culture, https://mki.wisc.edu/wp-content/uploads/sites/1100/2014/10/Keil-RACE_AND_ETHNICITY.pdf.

142 Keil, "Race and Ethnicity."

143 Albert Bernhardt Faust, *The German Element in the United States,* Vol. II: *The Influence of the German Element in the United States* (New York: Arno Press and *The New York Times*, 1969), 126; William E. Gienapp, *The Origins of the Republican Party, 1852-1856* (New York: Oxford University Press, 1987), 21.

144 James M. Bergquist, "The Forty-Eighters: Catalysts of German-American Politics," in *The German-American Encounter: Conflict and Cooperation Between Two Cultures, 1800-2000*, ed. Frank Trommler and Elliott Shore (New York: Berghahn, 2001), 26; Eric Foner, *Free Soil, Free Labor, Free Men: The Ideology of the Republican Party Before the Civil War* (New York: Oxford University Press, 1995), 292.

145 Tyler Anbinder, *Nativism and Slavery: The Northern Know Nothings and the Politics of the 1850s* (New York: Oxford University Press, 1992), 100-101.

146 Gienapp, *Origins of the Republican Party*, 76.

147 Gienapp, *Origins of the Republican Party*, 80, 81.

148 Bergquist, *Forty-Eighters: Catalysts,* 26; Carl Wittke, *Refugees of Revolution: The German Forty-Eighters in America* (Westport, CT: Greenwood, 1970), 195. In *The German-Language Press in America*

(Lexington: University of Kentucky Press, 1957), 6-7, Carl Wittke wrote that "the nineteenth-century German immigration was marked by a high rate of literacy, and it included a remarkably high percentage of well-educated Germans who made excellent journalists and who had a large constituency eager to read what they wrote."

149 Doris Kearns Goodwin, *Team of Rivals: The Political Genius of Abraham Lincoln* (New York: Simon & Schuster, 2005), 188, 189.

150 Bergquist, "Forty-Eighters: Catalysts," 28-29; Rolland Ray Lutz, "The German Revolutionary Student Movement, 1819-1833," *Central European History* 4, no. 3 (September 1971), https://www.jstor.org/stable/4545608. A student organization, the *Burschenschaft* was founded in Halle in 1814 and soon spread to the University of Jena and other universities across Germany. Its liberal-minded members advocated for human equality and the political unification of Germany.

151 James M. Bergquist, "The Mid-Nineteenth-Century Slavery Crisis and the German Americans," in *States of Progress: Germans and Blacks in America Over 300 Years*, ed. Randall M. Miller (Philadelphia: German Society of Pennsylvania, 1989), 66.

152 Chris DeRose, *The Presidents' War: Six American Presidents and the Civil War That Divided Them* (Guilford, CT: Lyons, 2014), 56.

153 Andrew R.L. Cayton, *Ohio: The History of a People* (Columbus: Ohio State University Press, 2002), 107.

154 Erica Hellerstein, "Letter from Germany: A Strange and Enduring Love Affair with the Antebellum South," Codastory, November 18, 2021, https://www.codastory.com/rewriting-history/uncle-toms-cabin-germany/; "German Brown-Eyed Porcelain Doll with Harriet Beecher Stowe Provenance," Theriault's, the Doll Masters, https://www.theriaults.com/german-brown-eyed-porcelain-doll-harriet-beecher-stowe-provenance.

155 Walter M. Tovell, *The Niagara Escarpment* (Toronto, ON: University of Toronto Press, 1978), 1, 3.

156 Richard Haw, *Engineering America: The Life and Times of John A. Roebling* (New York: Oxford University Press, 2020), 279; Hamilton Schuyler, *The Roeblings: A Century of Engineers, Bridge-Builders, and Industrialists* (Princeton, NJ: Princeton University Press, 1931), 109; Elizabeth McKinsey, *Niagara Falls: Icon of the American Sublime* (New York: Cambridge University Press, 1985), 253.

157 Robin Winks, *Canada and the United States: The Civil War Years* (Baltimore: Johns Hopkins University Press, 1960), 7.

158 Ginger Strand, *Inventing Niagara: Beauty, Power, and Lies* (New York: Simon & Schuster, 2008), 121; R.J.M. Blackett, "'Freemen to the Rescue!': Resistance to the Fugitive Slave Law of 1850," in *Passages to Freedom: The Underground Railroad in History and Memory*, ed. David W. Blight (Washington, DC: Smithsonian / New York: Collins, 2006), 134-135,146; Cheryl Janifer LaRoche, *Free Black Communities and the Underground Railroad: The Geography of Resistance* (Urbana: University of Illinois Press, 2014), 89.

159 Winks, *Canada and the United States*, 10; Nancy Butler, "Starting Anew: The Black Community of Early Niagara," in *Slavery and Freedom in Niagara,* ed. Michael Power and Nancy Butler, with Joy Ormsby (Niagara-on-the-Lake, ON: Niagara Historical Society, 2012), 48.

160 John N. Jackson, *The Mighty Niagara: One River—Two Frontiers*, with John Burtniak and Gregory P. Stein (Amherst, NY: Prometheus, 2003), 152, 155.

161 Donald Braider, *The Niagara*, Rivers of America Series (New York: Holt, Rinehart and Winston, 1972), 228; Strand, *Inventing Niagara*, 112.

162 Braider, *Niagara*, 226, 228; Karen Abbott, "The Daredevil of Niagara Falls," *Smithsonian Magazine*,

October 18, 2011, https://www.smithsonianmag.com/history/the-daredevil-of-niagara-falls-110492884/. An estimated 60,000 tourists visited Niagara Falls in 1850 because of the advent of the railroad, introduced in the US in 1827, and Canada, in 1836. See McKinsey, *Niagara Falls*, 253.

163 Clifford W. Zink, *The Roebling Legacy* (Princeton, NJ: Princeton Landmark Publications, 2011), 40; Haw, *Engineering America*, 320-321.

164 David P. Billington, *The Tower and the Bridge: The New Art of Structural Engineering* (Princeton, NJ: Princeton University Press, 1985), 75; Haw, *Engineering America*, 165, 169-170. In 1832, Roebling co-founded the town of Saxonburg in Butler County, Pennsylvania. His historic home in Saxonburg is listed on the National Register of Historic Places.

165 Schuyler, *Roeblings*, 117; Zink, *Roebling Legacy*, 50-51. Roebling's bridge at Niagara was replaced in 1897—forty-two years after it was built—because newer, heavier trains required a different mode of construction. See Schuyler, *Roeblings*, 123.

166 Billington, *Tower and the Bridge*, 77.

167 Haw, *Engineering America*, 88, 385.

168 Zink, *Roebling Legacy*, 25.

169 Strand, *Inventing Niagara*, 107-108, 115. Tubman was known to bribe toll collectors at the bridge so she could safely walk fugitive slaves across the lower, pedestrian level at night.

170 William H. Siener and Thomas A. Chambers, "Crossing to Freedom: Harriet Tubman and John A. Roebling's Suspension Bridge," *Western New York Heritage,* April 15, 2010, https://www.wnyheritage.org/content/crossing_to_freedom_harriet_tubman_and_john_a_roeblings_suspensi/index.html. On this particular trip, Tubman had secreted Joe Bailey and three other fugitive slaves aboard a train crossing Roebling's bridge into Canada. See Jeff Z. Klein, "Heritage Moments: Harriet Tubman Crosses the Niagara Falls Suspension Bridge," National Public Radio, June 6, 2016, https://www.wbfo.org/heritage-moments/2016-06-06/heritage-moments-harriet-tubman-crosses-the-niagara-falls-suspension-bridge.

171 James Oliver Horton and Lois E. Horton, *Slavery and the Making of America* (New York: Oxford University Press, 2005), 161-162. At the time of John Brown's famous raid in 1859, Harper's Ferry was in the western part of the State of Virginia. However, on June 20, 1863, President Abraham Lincoln signed a bill admitting West Virginia as the 35th state. See "West Virginia Statehood, June 20, 1863," Center for Legislative Archives, National Archives, https://www.archives.gov/legislative/features/west-virginia.

172 Horton and Horton, *Slavery and the Making of America*, 161-164, 166.

173 Bruce Levine, "Against All Slavery, Whether White or Black: German-Americans and the Irrepressible Conflict," in *Crosscurrents: African Americans, Africa, and Germany in the Modern World*, ed. David McBride, Leroy Hopkins, and C. Aisha Blackshire-Belay (Columbia, SC: Camden House, 1998), 53. In 1858, Forty-Eighter August Willich was asked to edit the *Cincinnati Republikaner*, which he did until 1861, at which time he joined the Union Army. Earlier, Willich had worked in Washington, DC, for the Federal Government, applying his knowledge of maps and charts to the Coastal and Geodetic Survey. See Loyd D. Easton, *Hegel's First American Followers* (Athens: Ohio University Press, 1966), 180, 190.

174 Levine, "Against All Slavery," 54.

175 Peter T. Lubrecht, Sr., *Carl Schurz, German-American Statesman: My Country, Right or Wrong*, America Through Time Series (Mount Pleasant, SC: Fonthill Media, 2019), 87; Donald Allendorf, *Your Friend, As Ever,*

A. Lincoln: How the Unlikely Friendship of Gustav Koerner and Abraham Lincoln Changed America (Gretna, LA: Pelican, 2014), 228; Carl Wittke, *Refugees of Revolution: The German Forty-Eighters in America* (Westport, CT: Greenwood, 1970), 213.

176 Lubrecht, *Carl Schurz*, 87-88; Hans L. Trefousse, "Abraham Lincoln and Carl Schurz," in *The German Forty-Eighters in the United States*, ed. Charlotte L. Brancaforte (New York: Peter Lang, 1989), 186. Recognizing the importance of the German vote, Lincoln in 1859 purchased the German-language newspaper called the *Illinois Staats-Anzeiger* (*Illinois State Gazette*) and hired the German-born editor, Theodore Canisius, to rally German-Americans toward Lincoln as the Republican candidate for president. See Harold Holzer, *Lincoln and the Power of the Press: The War for Public Opinion* (New York: Simon & Schuster, 2014), 186.

177 Michael Burlingame, *Abraham Lincoln: A Life*, Vol. 1 (Baltimore, MD: Johns Hopkins University Press, 2008), 680. In the slaveholding South, Lincoln carried just two counties, St. Louis and Gasconade, both in Missouri, where the population was primarily German. See Walter D. Kampoefner and Wolfgang Helbich, eds., *Germans in the Civil War: The Letters They Wrote Home*, Civil War America Series, trans. Susan Carter Vogel (Chapel Hill: University of North Carolina Press, 2006), 5.

178 Donald Allendorf, *Long Road to Liberty: The Odyssey of a German Regiment in the Yankee Army: The 15th Missouri Volunteer Infantry* (Kent, OH: Kent State University Press, 2006), xvii; Orville Vernon Burton, *The Age of Lincoln* (New York: Hill and Wang, 2007), 129; Richard Carwardine, *Lincoln: A Life of Purpose and Power* (New York: Knopf, 2006), 133; Doris Kearns Goodwin, *Team of Rivals: The Political Genius of Abraham Lincoln* (New York: Simon & Schuster, 2005), 272; Kamphoefner and Helbich, eds., *Germans in the Civil War*, 342-343; Lubrecht, *Carl Schurz*, 90; Martin W. Öfele, *True Sons of the Republic: European Immigrants in the Union Army*, Reflections on the Civil War Era Series (Westport, CT: Praeger, 2008), 31; Colin Woodard, *American Nations: A History of the Eleven Rival Regional Cultures of North America* (New York: Penguin, 2012), 188.

179 Margaret S. Creighton, *The Colors of Courage: Gettysburg's Forgotten History: Immigrants, Women, and African Americans in the Civil War's Defining Battle* (New York: Basic Books, 2005), 14; Brian Matthew Jordan, *A Thousand May Fall: Life, Death, and Survival in the Union Army* (New York: Liveright, 2021), 7.

180 Wilhelm Kaufmann, *The Germans in the American Civil War*, trans. Steven Rowan, ed. Don Heinrich Tolzmann, with Werner D. Mueller and Robert E. Ward (Carlisle, PA: John Kallmann, 1999), 76-77, 99.

181 Ezra J. Warner, *Generals in Blue: Lives of the Union Commanders* (Baton Rouge: Louisiana State University Press, 1972), xvii, 603; Bruce Levine, *The Spirit of 1848: German Immigrants, Labor Conflict, and the Coming of the Civil War* (Urbana: University of Illinois Press, 1992), 256. German-born soldiers also helped to maintain morale among the Union troops, wrote American historian Christian McWhirter, noting that "German bandsmen not only were plentiful but were considered musically superior to their English-speaking counterparts because of the preponderance of brass bands in their homeland. They were equally enthusiastic singers." See *Battle Hymns: The Power and Popularity of Music in the Civil War*, Civil War America Series (Chapel Hill: University of North Carolina Press, 2012), 128.

182 Hans A. Pohlsander, "Adolph von Steinwehr: A Neglected Civil War General," Loyola University Maryland and Notre Dame of Maryland University Library, https://loyolanotredamelib.org/php/report05/articles/pdfs/Report45Pohlsanderpp81-100.pdf.

183 Bruce Catton, *Glory Road*, Army of the Potomac Series (Garden City, NY: Doubleday, 1952), 175.

184 Barnett, Todd, "Carl Schurz," Historic Missourians, State Historical Society of Missouri, https://his-

toricmissourians.shsmo.org/carl-schurz. Before the Civil War broke out, Lincoln named Schurz ambassador to Spain. Anticipating the coming conflict, Schurz read numerous books on military tactics while he was stationed in Madrid to help ready himself for command.

185 Jenny Gesley, "The 'Lieber Code'—The First Modern Codification of the Laws of War," Library of Congress, April 24, 2018, https://blogs.loc.gov/law/2018/04/the-lieber-code-the-first-modern-codification-of-the-laws-of-war/.

186 Albert Bernhardt Faust, *The German Element in the United States*, Vol. II: *The Influence of the German Element in the United States* (New York: Arno Press and *The New York Times*, 1969), 168.

187 James G. Basker and Justine Ahlstrom, eds., "Abraham Lincoln and the Emancipation Proclamation." Gilder Lehrman Institute of American History, 2012. https://www.gilderlehrman.org/sites/default/files/inline-pdfs/GLI.LincEmProc.pdf.

188 Carwardine, *Lincoln*, 91, 201-211.

189 James Oakes, *The Crooked Path to Abolition: Abraham Lincoln and the Antislavery Constitution* (New York: Norton, 2021), 204.

190 Michael Beschloss, *Presidential Courage: Brave Leaders and How They Changed America, 1789-1989* (New York: Simon & Schuster, 2008), 109; Goodwin, *Team of Rivals*, 686.

Bibliography

Abbott, Karen. "The Daredevil of Niagara Falls." *Smithsonian Magazine*, October 18, 2011. https://www.smithsonianmag.com/history/the-daredevil-of-niagara-falls-110492884/.

"Adolf Cluss As the Dominant Architect for the Red Brick City." https://www.adolf-cluss.org/index.php?-sub=3.5&content=w&lang=en.

"Adolf Cluss Buildings: Sumner School." https://www.adolf-cluss.org/index.php?lang=en&topSub=washington&content=h&sub=3.5.59.

Allendorf, Donald. *Long Road to Liberty: The Odyssey of a German Regiment in the Yankee Army: The 15th Missouri Volunteer Infantry*. Kent, OH: Kent State University Press, 2006.

———. *Your Friend, As Ever, A. Lincoln: How the Unlikely Friendship of Gustav Koerner and Abraham Lincoln Changed America*. Gretna, LA: Pelican, 2014.

Anbinder, Tyler. *Nativism and Slavery: The Northern Know Nothings and the Politics of the 1850s*. New York: Oxford University Press, 1992.

Anderson, Kristen Layne. *Abolitionizing Missouri: German Immigrants and Racial Ideology in Nineteenth-Century America*. Antislavery, Abolition, and the Atlantic World Series. Baton Rouge: Louisiana State University Press, 2016.

"The Annexation of Texas, the Mexican-American War, and the Treaty of Guadalupe-Hidalgo, 1845-1848." Office of the Historian, Department of State. https://history.state.gov/milestones/1830-1860/texas-annexation.

Asch, Chris Myers, and George Derek Musgrove. *Chocolate City: A History of Race and Democracy in the Nation's Capital*. Chapel Hill: University of North Carolina Press, 2017.

Baptist, Edward E. *The Half Has Never Been Told: Slavery and the Making of American Capitalism*. New York: Basic Books, 2014.

Barnett, Todd. "Carl Schurz." Historic Missourians, State Historical Society of Missouri. https://historicmissourians.shsmo.org/carl-schurz.

Basker, James G., and Justine Ahlstrom, eds. "Abraham Lincoln and the Emancipation Proclamation." Gilder Lehrman Institute of American History, 2012. https://www.gilderlehrman.org/sites/default/files/inline-pdfs/GLI.LincEmProc.pdf.

Berlin, Ira. "Coming to Terms with Slavery in Twenty-First Century America." In *Slavery and Public History: The Tough Stuff of American Memory*, edited by James Oliver Horton and Lois E. Horton, 1-17. Chapel Hill: University of North Carolina Press, 2009.

———. *Generations of Captivity: A History of African-American Slaves*. Cambridge, MA: Belknap/Harvard University Press, 2003.

———. *Slaves Without Masters: The Free Negro in the Antebellum South*. New York: New Press, 1974. Bergquist, James M. "The Forty-Eighters: Catalysts of German-American Politics." In *The German-American Encounter: Conflict and Cooperation Between Two Cultures, 1800-2000*, edited by Frank Trommler and Elliott Shore, 22-36. New York: Berghahn, 2001.

———. "The Mid-Nineteenth-Century Slavery Crisis and the German Americans." In *States of Progress: Germans and Blacks in America Over 300 Years*, edited by Randall M. Miller, 55-71. Philadelphia: German Society of Pennsylvania, 1989.

Beschloss, Michael. *Presidential Courage: Brave Leaders and How They Changed America, 1789-1989*. New York: Simon & Schuster, 2008.

Billington, David P. *The Tower and the Bridge: The New Art of Structural Engineering*. Princeton, NJ: Princeton University Press, 1985.

Blackett, R.J.M. *The Captive's Quest for Freedom: Fugitive Slaves, the 1850 Fugitive Slave Law, and the Politics of Slavery*. Slavery Since Emancipation Series. New York: Cambridge University Press, 2018.

———. "'Freemen to the Rescue!': Resistance to the Fugitive Slave Law of 1850." In *Passages to Freedom: The Underground Railroad in History and Memory*, edited by David W. Blight, 133-147. Washington, DC: Smithsonian / New York: Collins, 2006.

Blumenbach, Johann Friedrich. *On the Natural Varieties of Mankind*. New York: Bergman, 1969. [First published in London, UK, by Longman, Green, Longman, Roberts, and Green, 1865, for the Anthropological Society of London.]

Bordewich, Fergus M. *Bound for Canaan: The Underground Railroad and the War for the Soul of America*. New York: Amistad, 2005.

Bourne, Jenny. "Slavery in the United States." *EH.Net Encyclopedia*, Economic History Association, March 26, 2008. https://eh.net/encyclopedia/slavery-in-the-united-states/.

Braider, Donald. *The Niagara*. Rivers of America Series. New York: Holt, Rinehart and Winston, 1972.

Bramble, Linda. *Black Fugitive Slaves in Early Canada*. Vanwell History Project Series. St. Catharines, ON: Vanwell, 1988.

Broadwater, Jeff. *James Madison: A Son of Virginia & a Founder of the Nation*. Chapel Hill: University of North Carolina Press, 2012.

Brookhiser, Richard. *Give Me Liberty: A History of America's Exceptional Idea*. New York: Basic Books, 2019.

Burlingame, Michael. *Abraham Lincoln: A Life*. Vol. 1. Baltimore, MD: Johns Hopkins University Press, 2008.

Burton, Orville Vernon. *The Age of Lincoln*. New York: Hill and Wang, 2007.

Butler, Nancy. "Starting Anew: The Black Community of Early Niagara." In *Slavery and Freedom in Niagara*, edited by Michael Power and Nancy Butler, 41-85. With Joy Ormsby. Niagara-on-the-Lake, ON: Niagara Historical Society, 2012.

Camp, Stephanie M.H. *Closer to Freedom: Enslaved Women and Everyday Resistance in the Plantation South*. Gender and American Culture Series. Chapel Hill: University of North Carolina Press, 2004.

Campbell, Stanley W. *The Slave Catchers: Enforcement of the Fugitive Slave Law, 1850-1860*. 2nd ed. Chapel Hill: University of North Carolina Press, 1970.

"The Caning of Senator Charles Sumner." United States Senate, Historical Highlights. https://www.senate.gov/artandhistory/history/minute/The_Caning_of_Senator_Charles_Sumner.htm.

Carwardine, Richard. *Lincoln: A Life of Purpose and Power*. New York: Knopf, 2006.

Catton, Bruce. *Glory Road*. Army of the Potomac Series. Garden City, NY: Doubleday, 1952.

Cayton, Andrew R.L. *Ohio: The History of a People*. Columbus: Ohio State University Press, 2002.

Collins, Gail. *William Henry Harrison*. American Presidents Series. New York: Henry Holt, 2012.

Costanzo, Adam. *George Washington's Washington: Visions for the National Capital in the Early American Republic*. Early American Places Series. Athens: University of Georgia Press, 2018.

Crapol, Edward P. *John Tyler: The Accidental President*. Chapel Hill: University of North Carolina Press, 2006.

Creighton, Margaret S. *The Colors of Courage: Gettysburg's Forgotten History: Immigrants, Women, and African Americans in the Civil War's Defining Battle*. New York: Basic Books, 2005.

Crothers, A. Glenn. *Quakers Living in the Lion's Mouth: The Society of Friends in Northern Virginia, 1730-1865*. Gainesville: University Press of Florida, 2012.

Cutter, Martha J. *The Illustrated Slave: Empathy, Graphic Narrative, and the Visual Culture of the Transatlantic Abolition Movement, 1800-1852*. Athens: University of Georgia Press, 2017.

Davis, Damani. "Slavery and Emancipation in the Nation's Capital." *Prologue Magazine* 42, no. 1 (spring 2010), National Archives. https://www.archives.gov/publications/prologue/2010/spring/dcslavery.html.

Davis, David Brion. *Inhuman Bondage: The Rise and Fall of Slavery in the New World*. New York: Oxford University Press, 2006.

———. *The Problem of Slavery in the Age of Emancipation*. New York: Knopf, 2014.

Davis, Harold E. *The Fledgling Province: Social and Cultural Life in Colonial Georgia, 1733-1776*. Williamsburg, VA: Omohundro Institute of Early American History and Culture / Chapel Hill: University of North Carolina Press, 1976.

Debrunner, Hans W. "Africa, Europe, and America: The Modern Roots from a European Perspective." In *Crosscurrents: African Americans, Africa, and Germany in the Modern World*, edited by David McBride, Leroy Hopkins, and C. Aisha Blackshire-Belay, 3-28. Columbia, SC: Camden House, 1998.

Delbanco, Andrew. *The War Before the War: Fugitive Slaves and the Struggle for America's Soul from the Revolution to the Civil War*. New York: Penguin, 2018.

DeRose, Chris. *The Presidents' War: Six American Presidents and the Civil War That Divided Them*. Guilford, CT: Lyons, 2014.

Dippel, Horst. *Germany and the American Revolution, 1770-1800: A Sociohistorical Investigation of Late Eighteenth-Century Political Thinking*. Translated by Bernhard A. Uhlendorf. Williamsburg, VA: Omohundro Institute of Early American History and Culture / Chapel Hill: University of North Carolina Press, 1977.

Easton, Loyd D. *Hegel's First American Followers*. Athens: Ohio University Press, 1966.

Efford, Alison Clark. *German Immigrants, Race, and Citizenship in the Civil War Era*. New York: Cambridge University Press, 2014.

"8th and H Streets NW - The Calvary Baptist Church." Streets of Washington, July 20, 2010. http://www.streetsofwashington.com/2010/07/8th-and-h-streets-nw-calvary-baptist.html.

Emery, Edwin. *The Press and America: An Interpretative History of the Mass Media*, 3rd ed. Englewood Cliffs, NJ: Prentice-Hall, 1972.

Essah, Patience. *A House Divided: Slavery and Emancipation in Delaware, 1638-1865*. Charlottesville: University Press of Virginia, 1996.

Faust, Albert Bernhardt. *The German Element in the United States*. Vol. II: *The Influence of the German Element in the United States*. New York: Arno Press and *The New York Times*, 1969.

Finkelman, Paul. "Slavery and Bondage in the 'Empire of Liberty.'" In *Northwest Ordinance: Essays on Its Formulation, Provisions, and Legacy*, edited by Frederick D. Williams, 61-95. East Lansing: Michigan State University Press, 1989.

———. *Slavery and the Founders: Race and Liberty in the Age of Jefferson*. Armonk, NY: M.E. Sharpe, 1996.

"The First Africans." Historic Jamestowne, National Park Service, Department of the Interior. https://historicjamestowne.org/history/the-first-africans/.

Fischer, David Hackett. *Albion's Seed: Four British Folkways in America*. New York: Oxford University Press, 1991.

Foner, Eric. *Free Soil, Free Labor, Free Men: The Ideology of the Republican Party Before the Civil War*. New York: Oxford University Press, 1995.

———. *Gateway to Freedom: The Hidden History of the Underground Railroad*. New York: Norton, 2015.

Foner, Philip S. "Alexander von Humboldt on Slavery in America." *Science & Society* 47, no. 3 (fall 1983). http://www.jstor.org/stable/40402500.

Forret, Jeff. "The Notorious 'Yellow House' That Made Washington, D.C. a Slavery Capital." *Smithsonian Magazine*, July 22, 2020. https://www.smithsonianmag.com/history/how-yellow-house-helped-make-washington-dc-slavery-capital-180975378/.

Franklin, John Hope, and Loren Schweninger. *Runaway Slaves: Rebels on the Plantation*. New York: Oxford University Press, 1999.

Freeman, Joanne B. *The Field of Blood: Violence in Congress and the Road to Civil War*. New York: Farrar, Straus and Giroux, 2018.

"Friedrich Kapp." *The Nation* 39, no. 1010 (November 6, 1884). https:en.wikisource.org/wiki/Friedrich_Kapp.

"Friedrich Tiedemann (1781-1861)." Universität Heidelberg, University Library. https://www.ub.uni-heidelberg.de/Englisch/helios/digi/anatomie/tiedemann.html.

Frost, Karolyn Smardz. *I've Got a Home in Glory Land: A Lost Tale of the Underground Railroad*. New York: Farrar, Straus and Giroux, 2008.

Fryer, Mary Beacock, and Christopher Dracott. *John Graves Simcoe, 1752-1806: A Biography*. Toronto, ON: Dundurn, 1998.

Gates, Jr., Henry Louis. "Did African-American Slaves Rebel?" The African Americans: Many Rivers to Cross, Public Broadcasting Service. https://www.pbs.org/wnet/african-americans-many-rivers-to-cross/history/did-african-american-slaves-rebel/.

Genovese, Eugene D. *Roll, Jordan, Roll: The World the Slaves Made*. New York: Pantheon, 1974.

"German Brown-Eyed Porcelain Doll with Harriet Beecher Stowe Provenance." Theriault's, the Doll Masters. https://www.theriaults.com/german-brown-eyed-porcelain-doll-harriet-beecher-stowe-provenance.

"Germantown Quaker Petition Against Slavery." National Park Service, Department of the Interior. https://www.nps.gov/articles/quakerpetition.htm.

Gesley, Jenny. "The 'Lieber Code'—The First Modern Codification of the Laws of War." Library of Congress, April 24, 2018. https://blogs.loc.gov/law/2018/04/the-lieber-code-the-first-modern-codification-of-the-laws-of-war/.

Gienapp, William E. *The Origins of the Republican Party, 1852-1856*. New York: Oxford University Press, 1987.

Goodwin, Doris Kearns. *Team of Rivals: The Political Genius of Abraham Lincoln*. New York: Simon & Schuster, 2005.

Gossett, Thomas F. *Race: The History of an Idea in America*. 2nd ed. New York: Oxford University Press, 1997.

Gould, Stephen Jay. "The Great Physiologist of Heidelberg—Friedrich Tiedemann—Brief Article." *Natural History*, July 1999. http://laboratoriogene.info/Ciencia_Hoje/Physiologist_Heidelberg.pdf.

Griffler, Keith P. *Front Line of Freedom: African Americans and the Forging of the Underground Railroad in the Ohio Valley*. Ohio River Valley Series. Lexington: University Press of Kentucky, 2004.

Hacker, J. David. "From '20. and Odd' to 10 Million: The Growth of the Slave Population in the United States." National Center for Biotechnology Information, National Library of Medicine, May 13, 2020. https://www.ncbi.nlm.nih.gov/pmc/articles/PMC7716878/.

Hansen, Thomas S. "Charles Follen: Brief Life of a Vigorous Reformer: 1796-1840." *Harvard Magazine*, September-October 2002. https://www.harvardmagazine.com/2002/09/charles-follen.html.

Harvey, Eleanor Jones. "Who Was Alexander von Humboldt?" *Smithsonian Magazine*, March 24, 2020. https://www.smithsonianmag.com/smithsonian-institution/who-was-alexander-von-humboldt-180974473/.

Haw, Richard. *Engineering America: The Life and Times of John A. Roebling*. New York: Oxford University Press, 2020.

Heinemann, Ronald L., John G. Kolp, Anthony S. Parent, Jr., and William G. Shade. *Old Dominion, New Commonwealth: A History of Virginia, 1607-2007*. Charlottesville: University of Virginia Press, 2007.

Hellerstein, Erica. "Letter from Germany: A Strange and Enduring Love Affair with the Antebellum South."

Codastory, November 18, 2021. https://www.codastory.com/rewriting-history/uncle-toms-cabin-germany/.

Henry, Natasha L. *Emancipation Day: Celebrating Freedom in Canada*. Toronto, ON: Dundurn, 2010.

Hill, Daniel G. *The Freedom-Seekers: Blacks in Early Canada*. Agincourt, ON: Book Society of Canada Limited, 1981.

Holland, Jesse J. *Black Men Built the Capitol: Discovering African-American History In and Around Washington, D.C.* Guilford, CT: Lyons, 2007.

Holzer, Harold. *Lincoln and the Power of the Press: The War for Public Opinion*. New York: Simon & Schuster, 2014.

Honeck, Mischa. *We Are the Revolutionists: German-Speaking Immigrants and American Abolitionists After 1848*. Race in the Atlantic World, 1700-1900 Series. Athens: University of Georgia Press, 2011.

Horton, James Oliver, and Lois E. Horton. *Slavery and the Making of America*. New York: Oxford University Press, 2005.

"*Illinois Staats-Zeitung*." Academic Dictionaries and Encyclopedias. https://en-academic.com/dic.nsf/enwiki/11528635.

Jackson, John N. *The Mighty Niagara: One River—Two Frontiers*. With John Burtniak and Gregory P. Stein. Amherst, NY: Prometheus, 2003.

Jacobs, Harriet. *Incidents in the Life of a Slave Girl: Written by Herself*. New York: Barnes & Noble Classics, 2005.

Jones, Jeannette Eileen. "On the Brain of the Negro: Race, Abolitionism, and Friedrich Tiedemann's Scientific Discourse on the African Diaspora." In *Germany and the Black Diaspora: Points of Contact, 1250-1914*, edited by Mischa Honeck, Martin Klimke, and Anne Kuhlmann, 134-152. New York: Berghahn, 2013.

Jorati, Julia. "Leibniz on Slavery and the Ownership of Human Beings." *Journal of Modern Philosophy* 1, no. 1 (December 4, 2019). https://jmphil.org/articles/10.32881/jomp.45/.

Jordan, Brian Matthew. *A Thousand May Fall: Life, Death, and Survival in the Union Army*. New York: Liveright, 2021.

Jordan, Winthrop D. *White Over Black: American Attitudes Toward the Negro, 1550-1812*. Williamsburg, VA: Omohundro Institute of Early American History and Culture / Chapel Hill: University of North Carolina Press, 1968.

Kamphoefner, Walter D., and Wolfgang Helbich, eds. *Germans in the Civil War: The Letters They Wrote Home*. Civil War America Series. Translated by Susan Carter Vogel. Chapel Hill: University of North Carolina Press, 2006.

Kaufmann, Wilhelm. *The Germans in the American Civil War*. Translated by Steven Rowan. Edited by Don Heinrich Tolzmann. With Werner D. Mueller and Robert E. Ward. Carlisle, PA: John Kallmann, 1999.

Keil, Hartmut. "Race and Ethnicity: Slavery and the German Radical Tradition." Presentation given in Madison, Wisconsin, February 3, 1999, sponsored by the Max Kade Institute for German-American Studies and the Center for the History of Print Culture. https://mki.wisc.edu/wp-content/uploads/sites/1100/2014/10/Keil-RACE_AND_ETHNICITY.pdf.

Kelly, Jack. *Heaven's Ditch: God, Gold, and Murder on the Erie Canal*. New York: St. Martin's, 2016.

Kindy, Dave. "Va. Church Where George Washington Prayed Honors Its Enslaved Builders." *The Washington Post*, March 15, 2023. https://www.washingtonpost.com/history/2023/03/15/pohick-church-george-washington-enslaved/.

Klein, Jeff Z. "Heritage Moments: Harriet Tubman Crosses the Niagara Falls Suspension Bridge." National Public Radio, June 6, 2016. https://www.wbfo.org/heritage-moments/2016-06-06/heritage-moments-harriet-tubman-crosses-the-niagara-falls-suspension-bridge.

"Landmark Legislation: The District of Columbia Compensated Emancipation Act." United States Senate. https://www.senate.gov/artandhistory/history/common/generic/DCEmancipationAct.htm.

LaRoche, Cheryl Janifer. *Free Black Communities and the Underground Railroad: The Geography of Resistance*.

Urbana: University of Illinois Press, 2014.

Levine, Bruce. "'Against All Slavery, Whether White or Black': German-Americans and the Irrepressible Conflict." In *Crosscurrents: African Americans, Africa, and Germany in the Modern World*, edited by David McBride, Leroy Hopkins, and C. Aisha Blackshire-Belay, 53-64. Columbia, SC: Camden House, 1998.

———. *The Spirit of 1848: German Immigrants, Labor Conflict, and the Coming of the Civil War*. Urbana: University of Illinois Press, 1992.

Lewis, Tom. *Washington: A History of Our National City*. New York: Basic Books, 2015.

Lubrecht, Peter T., Sr. *Carl Schurz, German-American Statesman: My Country, Right or Wrong*. America Through Time Series. Mount Pleasant, SC: Fonthill Media, 2019.

Lutz, Rolland Ray. "The German Revolutionary Student Movement, 1819-1833." *Central European History* 4, no. 3 (September 1971). https://www.jstor.org/stable/4545608.

Mann, Lina. "Building the White House." Slavery in the President's Neighborhood, White House Historical Association, January 3, 2020. https://www.whitehousehistory.org/building-the-white-house.

Marten, James. *Texas Divided: Loyalty and Dissent in the Lone Star State, 1856-1874*. Lexington: University Press of Kentucky, 1990.

May, Henry F. *The Enlightenment in America*. New York: Oxford University Press, 1976.

Mayer, Henry. *All on Fire: William Lloyd Garrison and the Abolition of Slavery*. New York: Norton, 2008.

McKinsey, Elizabeth. *Niagara Falls: Icon of the American Sublime*. New York: Cambridge University Press, 1985.

McWhirter, Christian. *Battle Hymns: The Power and Popularity of Music in the Civil War*. Civil War America Series. Chapel Hill: University of North Carolina Press, 2012.

Meacham, Jon. *American Lion: Andrew Jackson in the White House*. New York: Random House, 2008.

Metaxas, Eric. *Amazing Grace: William Wilberforce and the Heroic Campaign to End Slavery*. New York: HarperOne, 2008.

Mintz, Steven. "Historical Context: The Constitution and Slavery." History Resources, Gilder Lehrman Institute of American History. https://www.gilderlehrman.org/history-resources/teaching-resource/historical-context-constitution-and-slavery.

"Missouri Compromise Ushers in New Era for the Senate." United States Senate, Historical Highlights. https://www.senate.gov/artandhistory/history/minute/Missouri_Compromise.htm.

Morgan, Philip D. "Virginia Slavery in Atlantic Context, 1550-1650." In *Virginia 1619: Slavery and Freedom in the Making of English America*, edited by Paul Musselwhite, Peter C. Mancall, and James Horn, 85-107. Williamsburg, VA: Omohundro Institute of Early American History and Culture / Chapel Hill: University of North Carolina Press, 2019.

Morris, Thomas D. *Southern Slavery and the Law, 1619-1860*. Studies in Legal History Series. Chapel Hill: University of North Carolina Press, 1996.

Newman, Peter C. *Hostages to Fortune: The United Empire Loyalists and the Making of Canada*. Toronto, ON: Simon & Schuster Canada, 2016.

Oakes, James. *The Crooked Path to Abolition: Abraham Lincoln and the Antislavery Constitution*. New York: Norton, 2021.

Öfele, Martin W. *True Sons of the Republic: European Immigrants in the Union Army*. Reflections on the Civil War Era Series. Westport, CT: Praeger, 2008.

Parkinson, Robert G. *Thirteen Clocks: How Race United the Colonies and Made the Declaration of Independence*. Williamsburg, VA: Omohundro Institute of Early American History and Culture / Chapel Hill: University of North Carolina Press, 2021.

Philbrick, Nathaniel. *Travels with George: In Search of Washington and His Legacy*. New York: Viking, 2021.

Piersen, William D. *Black Yankees: The Development of an Afro-American Subculture in Eighteenth-Century*

New England. Amherst: University of Massachusetts Press, 1988.

Pohlsander, Hans A. "Adolph von Steinwehr: A Neglected Civil War General." Loyola University Maryland and Notre Dame of Maryland University Library. https://loyolanotredamelib.org/php/report05/articles/pdfs/Report45Pohlsanderpp81-100.pdf.

Power, Michael. "Simcoe and Slavery." In *Slavery and Freedom in Niagara*, edited by Michael Power and Nancy Butler, 9-39. With Joy Ormsby. Niagara-on-the-Lake, ON: Niagara Historical Society, 2012.

Rael, Patrick. *Eighty-Eight Years: The Long Death of Slavery in the United States, 1777-1865.* Race in the Atlantic World, 1700-1900 Series. Athens: University of Georgia Press, 2015.

Ross, Marc Howard. *Slavery in the North: Forgetting History and Recovering Memory.* Philadelphia: University of Pennsylvania Press, 2018.

Rowan, Steven. "Emil Preetorius (1827-1905)." *Missouri Encyclopedia.* https://missouriencyclopedia.org/people/preetorius-emil.

Schöberl, Ingrid. "Franz Daniel Pastorius and the Foundation of Germantown." In *Germans to America: 300 Years of Immigration, 1683-1983*, edited by Günter Moltmann, 16-24. Translated by Robert W. Culverhouse. Stuttgart, DEU: Institute for Foreign Cultural Relations, 1982.

Schuyler, Hamilton. *The Roeblings: A Century of Engineers, Bridge-Builders, and Industrialists.* Princeton, NJ: Princeton University Press, 1931.

Secor, Robert, ed. *Pennsylvania 1776.* University Park: Pennsylvania State University Press, 1976.

Sheehan, James J. *German History, 1770-1866.* Oxford History of Modern Europe Series. Oxford, UK: Clarendon, 1993.

Sibley, Marilyn M. "Douai, Carl Daniel Adolph (1819-1888)." *Handbook of Texas*, Texas State Historical Association. https://www.tshaonline.org/handbook/entries/douai-carl-daniel-adolph.

Siener, William H., and Thomas A. Chambers. "Crossing to Freedom: Harriet Tubman and John A. Roebling's Suspension Bridge." *Western New York Heritage*, April 15, 2010. https://www.wnyheritage.org/content/crossing_to_freedom_harriet_tubman_and_john_a_roeblings_suspensi/index.html.

Soderlund, Jean R. *Quakers and Slavery: A Divided Spirit.* Princeton, NJ: Princeton University Press, 1985.

Stampp, Kenneth M. *The Peculiar Institution: Slavery in the Ante-Bellum South.* New York: Knopf, 1956.

Strand, Ginger. *Inventing Niagara: Beauty, Power, and Lies.* New York: Simon & Schuster, 2008.

Thomas, Velma Maia. *Lest We Forget: The Passage from Africa into the Twenty-First Century.* Bellevue, WA: Becker & Mayer, 2018.

Tovell, Walter M. *The Niagara Escarpment.* Toronto, ON: University of Toronto Press, 1978.

Trefousse, Hans L. "Abraham Lincoln and Carl Schurz." In *The German Forty-Eighters in the United States*, edited by Charlotte L. Brancaforte, 179-201. New York: Peter Lang, 1989.

Vlach, John Michael. "Above Ground on the Underground Railroad: Places of Flight and Refuge." In *Passages to Freedom: The Underground Railroad in History and Memory*, edited by David W. Blight, 95-115. Washington, DC: Smithsonian / New York: Collins, 2006.

Waite, Kevin. *West of Slavery: The Southern Dream of a Transcontinental Empire.* David J. Weber Series in the New Borderlands History. Chapel Hill: University of North Carolina Press, 2021.

Walls, Laura Dassow. *The Passage to Cosmos: Alexander von Humboldt and the Shaping of America.* Chicago, IL: University of Chicago Press, 2009.

Walvin, James. *Freedom: The Overthrow of the Slave Empires.* London, UK: Robinson, 2019.

Warner, Ezra J. *Generals in Blue: Lives of the Union Commanders.* Baton Rouge: Louisiana State University Press, 1972.

"West Virginia Statehood, June 20, 1863." Center for Legislative Archives, National Archives. https://www.archives.gov/legislative/features/west-virginia.

White, Deborah Gray. "Simple Truths: Antebellum Slavery in Black and White." In *Passages to Freedom:*

The Underground Railroad in History and Memory, edited by David W. Blight, 33-65. Washington, DC: Smithsonian / New York: Collins, 2006.

Widmer, Ted. *Martin Van Buren*. American Presidents Series. New York: Henry Holt, 2005.

Wilson, Carol. *Freedom at Risk: The Kidnapping of Free Blacks in America, 1780-1865*. Lexington: University Press of Kentucky, 1994.

Winks, Robin W. *The Blacks in Canada: A History*. 2nd ed. Montréal, QC: McGill-Queen's University Press, 2008.

———. *Canada and the United States: The Civil War Years*. Baltimore, MD: Johns Hopkins University Press, 1960.

Wittke, Carl. *The German-Language Press in America*. Lexington: University of Kentucky Press, 1957.

———. *Refugees of Revolution: The German Forty-Eighters in America*. Westport, CT: Greenwood, 1970.

Woodard, Colin. *American Nations: A History of the Eleven Rival Regional Cultures of North America*. New York: Penguin, 2012.

Wood, Betty. *Slavery in Colonial America, 1619-1776*. African American History Series. Lanham, MD: Rowman & Littlefield, 2005.

Wust, Klaus, and Heinz Moos, eds. *Three Hundred Years of German Immigrants in North America, 1683-1983: Their Contributions to the Evolution of the New World*. Munich, DEU: Heinz Moos, 1983.

Young, Ralph. *Dissent: The History of an American Idea*. New York: New York University Press, 2015.

Zammito, John H. "Policing Polygeneticism in Germany, 1775 (Kames,) Kant, and Blumenbach." In *The German Invention of Race*, edited by Sara Eigen and Mark Larrimore, 35-54. SUNY Philosophy and Race Series. Albany: State University of New York Press, 2006.

Zink, Clifford W. *The Roebling Legacy*. Princeton, NJ: Princeton Landmark Publications, 2011.

Image Credits

Chapter One
United States Public Domain {{PD-US}}: Johann Friedrich Blumenbach
Creative Commons Attribution 3.0 Unported: Map of the Original 13 Colonies; Pastorius Monument

Chapter Two
United States Public Domain {{PD-US}}: James Madison; *Writing the Declaration of Independence, 1776*

Chapter Three
United States Public Domain {{PD-US}}: Map of Delaware and Maryland

Chapter Four
United States Public Domain {{PD-US}}: James Monroe

Chapter Five
Creative Commons Attribution-Share Alike 3.0 Unported: Map of Province of Upper Canada
Creative Commons Attribution-Share Alike 4.0 International: William Wilberforce (Stephencdickson)

Chapter Six
United States Public Domain {{PD-US}}: Martin Van Buren

Chapter Seven
United States Public Domain {{PD-US}}: Friedrich Hecker; Adolf Cluss

Chapter Eight
Creative Commons Attribution-Share Alike 4.0 International: North Star (Joshua Wiese; cropped)
United States Public Domain {{PD-US}}: *Slave Hunt, Dismal Swamp, Virginia*

Chapter Nine
Creative Commons Attribution-Share Alike 4.0 International: Kansas-Nebraska Territories (Golbez)
United States Public Domain {{PD-US}}: James Buchanan

Chapter Ten
United States Public Domain {{PD-US}}: Slave Catcher's Role; *Armenia* Steamboat

Printed in the USA
CPSIA information can be obtained
at www.ICGtesting.com
LVHW070902071023
760459LV00017B/234